COUPLES THAI MASSAGE

Your Guide to Sharing (Mutually) Incredible Loving Touch

SHAI PLONSKI

Published by Still Light Center, School of Thai Massage

www.StillLightCenter.com

DISCLAIMER:

Important Information to Read Before Beginning

The information contained in this book is for informational and recreational purposes only, and should not be used to replace professional medical advice. People who purchase this book are solely responsible for how they choose to utilize this content.

This book and information contained herein should not be relied on in diagnosing or treating a medical condition. It is best to seek advice and attention from your physician or qualified healthcare professional. Always consult your physician before beginning a new treatment or fitness program. However, with that in mind, if used for the purposes of promoting and sharing relaxation, kindness, and compassion in a manner that respects and honors the abilities and limitations of both you and the person to whom you are giving the massage, then be prepared for outstanding results.

TAKE YOUR MASSAGE TO THE NEXT LEVEL!

Learn Couples Thai Massage and everything in this book with our online course.

- ✓ Step-by-step guidance
- ✓ Done-for-you massages to share from 15 min. up to 1 hour
- ✓ Incredible support
- ✓ Visit https://www.stilllightcenter.com/online-massage-courses or email info@stilllightcenter.com to get started

TABLE OF CONTENTS

INTRODUCTION

Unlocking the Secrets of Compassionate Loving Touch

Welcome! Thank you for coming along on this life-changing adventure of learning Couples Thai Yoga Massage. It is a practice that can produce amazing results regarding the quality of your relationship and love life, as well as your mutual health and well-being.

The techniques shared herein can be learned quickly and at a very high level so that you can provide each other with high-quality massages that address pain, tension, and stress in the shoulders, back, neck, legs, feet, head, and more.

It can also help deepen your connection and open your heart and body to your partner, to healing, to yourself, and all that you are capable of. Such is the power of meditative, loving, and compassionate touch! Although ground zero might be sharing and learning this massage with your life partner or your boyfriend or girlfriend, the methods shared herein can also be used to massage friends, family members, or any person in need with whom you want to share these practices.

One of the wonderful benefits behind everything you learn herein is that giving this massage is such a pleasure for you—the giver—which will mean wanting to give it to as many people as possible.

Recently, I have been thinking a lot about what this book may mean to you and what the power of touch has meant to me and the thousands of students I have taught.

Once you learn these valuable skills and put them to great use, there may be no turning back. Your life will be beneficially changed forever. In putting this book and course together, I believe that I know why.

There is a major movement afoot that has been building for decades, but which has really taken off during the past several years. It is a movement dedicated to taking control of our health and our well-being.

Visiting the doctor is essential for many, if not all of us; however, we now view this as but one piece of the puzzle. As health care becomes increasingly expensive for individuals and the companies and governments that invest in it, and with all of the resources now available on the internet and in our neighborhoods regarding how to take better care of ourselves, people have become increasingly invested in one sweet word: nutrition.

We often associate nutrition with the food that we eat. Of course, if we eat well, we will be healthier. However, I want to think more broadly about optimal nutrition and associate it with the word and expression of nurturing. When we exercise regularly, we feed our muscles, bodies, and our hearts with all kinds of good nutrition. If we read good books, we feed our minds. If we meditate, do yoga, make conscious lifestyle choices, or take walks on the beach, we feed our mind and body connection.

Fortunately, an increasing number of people now understand just how important it is to feed ourselves well and nurture all of the parts of us that make us human, and they are taking an active interest in finding ways to do that.

One area that is still so often overlooked, but which is as important as all of these approaches to nurturing ourselves, is with touch. It is a very interesting time when it comes to touch.

On the one hand, we are becoming a society that is more open to touch. I remember when my male friends and I began hugging in public in the 90s and how this was viewed as weird. Now, we see it everywhere between men, women, and all people across all cultures. However, hugs, kisses, and caresses are just the tip of the iceberg when it comes to loving touch and nonsexual intimacy.

At the same time, there has been a pushback against touch as a result of the many inappropriate ways in which people have taken advantage and have been taken advantage of. The "Me Too" and "Time's Up" movements have helped raise awareness and made people conscious of the need for consent when it comes to touch.

If we meditate, do yoga, make conscious lifestyle choices, or take walks on the beach, we feed our mind and body connection. Fortunately, an increasing number of people now understand just how important it is to feed ourselves well and nurture all of the parts of us that make us human, and they are taking an active interest in finding ways to do that.

My belief is that when compassionate touch—and massage—is done in a way that includes both consent and compassion, its power to heal and connect is profound.

With all of the pressure that we place on ourselves, with all of the stress that we face, with all of the ways in which we unconsciously use our bodies, with all of the responsibility that we take on, and with all of the surprising and bad news that hits us throughout our day, we cannot help but be affected.

On some level, this hurts, and there is both an emotional and physical toll, regardless of whether these things affect us directly or whether it is something that we see on the news to which we feel connected. This kind of non-stop onslaught has an impact on our bodies and health whether we realize it or not. It puts stress on our shoulders, tightens our backs, causes us to close in, and forces our bodies to shrink.

When we add to this the natural impact of aging that also causes us to lose some of our mobility and flexibility, then these issues are only magnified. I have seen again and again how people are in pain. It may be physical, emotional, or both. It may be mild, dull, or simply a pain that we would rather not have. We can handle it, so we either put up with it or ignore it. For a long time—perhaps even for decades—we can get away with it. However, then there is the day when all of this catches up to us and the pain becomes a severe backache, a strong neck pain, or some other kind of ailment.

When that occurs, we have a big enough problem that we can no longer ignore it. For many of us, after watching our parents and grandparents live with these issues, we may silently accept this as our fate and simply chalk it up to the price of getting older.

Well, I am here to tell you that it does not have to be this way. It is entirely possible to rid ourselves of the mild aches and pains that we feel and prevent them from ever becoming bigger problems down the road. If you are reading this and you have some of those bigger problems, then it is also very possible to manage them and potentially eliminate them. That is a big part of why we are learning to eat better and embrace all of those aspects of nutrition. However, if we don't bring skilled and regular massage built on loving, compassionate touch into our lives, then we are missing an essential piece of the puzzle.

Let's put this another way. Imagine learning some skilled and compassionate massage techniques with your partner. Imagine that you started taking turns massaging each other for 20 or 30 minutes per week—or even longer! What kind of impact do you think that would have on your life when you engage in this kind of exchange for a month or year? How about five years or even 50 years? How would that improve both of your bodies now and for the future? How would that nurture (there's that word again) your relationship? How might that help you communicate how deeply you care about one another?

How might that impact your love life? If you are brand new to massage, yet, you believe that this would lead to a pretty amazing positive change in your life and the people you care about, then I have some great news for you. I have to let you in on a little secret. When it comes to being able to give this kind of touch, you already possess more knowledge and skill than you might be aware of. Allow me to explain. You see, I was blessed to have a daughter ten years into my massage teaching career.

It was such a revelation to see her go from a total newborn without a clue of how to be in the world to someone figuring things out at such a rapid pace in so many amazing ways.

One of the very first things she learned several days into her life was that there is a space between her hand and her mouth. From there, she learned that when she moved her hand to her mouth, she was able to close that gap. So it began: a love affair with touch. The way she first learned about pretty much anything was through touch.

This process is not unique to her, and we—her parents—did not do anything specific to encourage it. Touch is the first sense we develop, starting when we are still inside of our mothers, and so much about what we learn and how we engage with the world at the start of our lives is through touch. It is only later in life that many of us prioritize other senses to help experience the richness of life, including beautiful sunsets, delicious sandwiches, favorite songs, and the smell of our favorite flowers.

However, we all have a finely tuned sense of touch. We use it every day, even though for many of us, it's more subconscious than our other senses. Interestingly, there was a time when it dominated how we interact with the world, as well as how we knew that we are loved, safe, and cared for. As a result, I am confident that with a little practice and the right system to help, you can give a highly compassionate, skilled, and nurturing massage. Best of all, it will not take long at all!

My job is to teach you to tap into the skills that you already know and put them into a system that is at least as good, as fun, and as healthy to give as it is to receive.

In fact, when I first started out in the world of massage over 20 years ago, I never thought that I would make a career out of this. There really is just one reason I did and have continued to stick with it, which is that I am able to do something that is often better to give than it is to receive. The kind of compassionate touch that I am going to teach you may resemble what you think of as massage, but it is also completely different. This method teaches you to massage mostly without your hands and thumbs. It will teach you to rely on your forearms, your feet, and your whole body instead.

You'll also bring customized movements—or stretches—to the experience, both for the individual giving and the individual receiving. My belief and experience has taught me that muscles are meant to move. Many of the issues that we have are a product of either a lack of movement or too much movement in a way that is not supportive or in alignment with our body's best ways to move. As a result, when we move our body and muscles in a healthy way, both as a giver and receiver of massage, we are doing what our body is meant to do, which makes our bodies happier and healthier.

When we combine customized movements with massage techniques built on a platform of compassionate touch, the feelings of relaxation, ease, and letting go of tension are exponentially greater. Similarly, the experiences of relaxation, revitalization, and pain leaving the body become much more profound, as does the feeling of love and appreciation that you have for the person helping provide you with that experience.

Even if you don't have any experience giving massages, you can learn to do so quickly at a very high level. You can expect your partner to give you feedback such as, "Your massage helped me feel two inches taller" or "Now I feel ten years younger!" Perhaps they will say that it filled them up with love and appreciation for you as the stress melted out of their body.

Ultimately, it is all here for you in this training, and if you give it a few hours of your time, you will develop a skill for life. That is, a skill that you'll be able to use for the rest of your life and one that enhances the quality of being alive for your partner, your family, your friends, and yourself. Moreover, as good as it is to receive this kind of experience (and it really is that good!), it also needs to be at least that good to give. Otherwise, what's the point?

If we don't love giving this and if we don't receive amazing benefits from the experience, then we may try it for a little while, but eventually we will lose interest and move on to the next thing. If it does not give both you and your partner incredible and instant rewards, then you'll find something else that does. Accordingly, that is what this book and program are about. This course is here to offer you the missing link in nutrition and in nurturing your body, mind, energy, and (if you believe in it) soul. By opening up to the love and compassion that already exists inside of you and expressing it as a highly skilled massage, it also makes you more available to feel the love that you have for your partner and vice versa. This love can be more easily shared through lovemaking and whatever else moves you in how you want to connect with your partner.

As such, this book and accompanying video course are here to help you improve your relationships.

By giving this massage regularly, you will help each other and the people you care about get rid of tension and pain, forget about their troubles, and feel good, relaxed, and at ease. It is a path to a better life that is available to everyone. Accordingly, you and whoever you are sharing this with will receive immense benefits. This is because touch is a universal skill, and we can all access it to help make a better life for our planet, loved ones, and ourselves. Needless to say, I am excited to begin, and I hope you are too!

Before we start, I can hear the most common question and most common doubt from a mile away. In fact, when discussing this book and program with friends and family, they all had the same question: is it really possible to learn something like this without a teacher present?

The answer is a resounding yes! Err, I mean no!

Actually, the answer to this question depends on who you think your teacher is. If you believe that I am your only teacher, then the answer is no. I do not need to be present for you to be able to excel at this course. Now, this does not mean that I will not be available to answer your questions. This is a course that I teach all over the world, including regularly at the famed Kripalu Center, a yoga retreat center in Lenox, Massachusetts. As you dive in, if you want to learn and refine your skills in person and on retreat, that option is available to you.

However, when you expand your idea of who your teacher is and embrace all of the resources available to you, then you will quickly see that you have everything you need to learn this massage in the comfort of your own home.

From that point of view, what I am asking you to accept is that you have more than one teacher who will help you and your partner learn this at a really high level. In fact, with the system I teach, whether that be at home or in person, my approach is that your primary teacher is your partner. If you give these techniques to many people, then you will have numerous teachers who will show you the way. I will also help you realize that you are your own teacher. Accordingly, you will be tapping in to the innate knowledge that I mentioned earlier.

The first thing that you are going to learn is called the "four pillars," which are at the heart of everything we do, and which are going to teach you what we already discussed. You already know what to do because of how experienced you are at developing a sensitivity to touch.

As a result, you will be your own teacher when it comes to learning how to give this. Furthermore, all of the written material that is presented to you here, which includes detailed explanations and variations regarding how to give everything with safety, support, and care is going to help teach you. If you choose, you can also purchase the accompanying video course, which includes done-for-you massages of varying lengths and over 12 hours of detailed, step-by-step guidance to learn the system and put it into practice at very high level. For this video course, visit www.stilllightcenter.com/online-massage-courses.

It is all designed with couples in mind, along with the added focus on how to help make this a regular aspect of your life. As a result, you can practice the material presented here as four mini-massages, or one longer one. The mini-massages take 15-20 minutes to give and are the kind of things that you can give and receive at least once per week.

The first part is a massage with your partner lying on their side so that you can target their neck, arm, back, and legs. The second part is a massage with them lying face down so that you can give a deep back massage along with an additional massage for their feet and legs. Part three has them on their back for a dynamic stretch that opens up the back, sacrum, hips, and legs. Part four addresses the head, neck, and shoulders.

Put it all together for the full-blown 60-minute experience and you will have a date night to beat all date nights!

You have all kinds of teachers and support to help you learn something that is going to be fun, interesting, perhaps challenging (but not too difficult), and an absolutely life-changing ride. Are you with me? Are you ready to get started? Here we go! ☺

PART 1:

PREPARING FOR COUPLES THAI MASSAGE

CHAPTER 1: The First Three Pillars of Thai Massage

At the heart of this system are the four fundamental pillars, which are the tools that allow you to become your own teacher. Every technique and part of the massage you learn is an extension of these four pillars. You can see the four pillars come together with everything you give. As a result, the more comfortable you are with the four pillars, the easier it will be to become comfortable with the massage itself. The whole point of the four pillars is that you can quickly become your own teacher, and you and your body will know exactly what to do.

The four pillars will help you immensely to practice in a manner that emphasizes safety and respect to the highest degree for both you and your partner. To practice safely means that there is never any strain on your body. Every session is part of a long-term plan so that you can keep practicing for 50 years or more. This is entirely possible when you pay attention to your movements and find ways to practice effectively, with appropriate pressure in ways that are in harmony with your body.

In this chapter, we'll begin with the first three pillars of the massage. These pillars are all about the giver and are here to help make the experience as enjoyable and beneficial possible. One of the only fundamental rules in my school is that we want to make giving the massage at least as good (if not 10 times as good) for the person giving as it is for the person receiving.

These pillars are the building blocks that help you to do that. They will help you to use your entire body with great awareness. They are here to help coach you so that everything you do comes from your core and your heart.

You do not have to practice in the exact manner that I show you in the descriptions or videos. I am practicing in a way that is comfortable for me and provides a general approach that may work for many of you. However, your guide is the four pillars. Make any adaptations to suit your body and your session, even if that includes taking out any techniques that you do not feel comfortable with. Remember what we discussed before. This session has to be at least as good to give as it is to receive. This will make it best for us as the giver, but the fact is that the better you feel, the better your partner will feel as well.

From your partner's point of view, safe practice involves bringing them into positions that they are comfortable with. Remember to always check in at the beginning and have a clear picture of their flexibility and any restrictions or injuries. This is true even if you are helping your life partner of 20 years! Continue reading and you will see many ways in which we are going to help you protect and support your partner and honor them as your most important teacher.

The First Pillar: Being Mindful / Meditation & Metta (The Spirit of Loving, Kindness & Compassion)

At the heart of this course and unlocking the secrets of universal touch is this first pillar. In so many ways, it is the only pillar and only thing we need to be successful at creating an amazing experience. You may think of this as paying attention, meditation, or whatever makes sense for you. However, this is the secret to giving a great massage. It is only normal that our attention is going to wander at times while we massage, but the key is what you do once you notice that it has wandered.

During the massage, we want to be as alert and attentive as possible. Being alert will occur in two ways: by making yourself comfortable and making your partner comfortable. When you notice your attention wandering off to different things, take note and guide it back. You can guide it back to your massage, and you can also think about your partner. Think about something that you love about them, whether it is a story from your shared past, something they do, or something that helps you feel good about this wonderful person in front of you. To help you pay attention, I recommend coming to your breath. Be aware of your inhale and exhale. We breathe every second, and when we notice our breath, we are noticing something happening in the present. For this reason, among many others, it is a great way to help bring us into the moment. The more you pay attention to your breath, the more that your breath tends to relax and become longer without any force. As that happens naturally, we relax a little more, our tensions have an outlet to release, and we feel better effortlessly.

The more you attempt to pay attention—even if it is for one breath—the more you feel good. It is that good feeling that you want to make an increasingly present part of your life. That good feeling is already within us; it is the positive energy of every moment. It is what is called "metta" or loving, kindness, and compassion. Whether you feel it or not right now, it is inside you. It is part of you just as much as your hair color or the shape of your features. The way your body works to help get better, heal, protect itself, and learn something are all examples of metta. Think about it: our body is comprised of at least 50 trillion cells. Each of these cells is an individual unit with an end and beginning. It has its own power source (i.e., the mitochondria), unique shape, and unique ability.

It is an individual unit just as we are all individuals making ourselves heard and surviving in this world. Yet, each one of these cells will also support the whole and the other cells in your body when there is a need.

For example, if you hurt your right shoulder, your left side will take on some of the pain to make it's easier for the right. This happens without question time and time again. No matter the issue, the whole body works together to overcome challenges. That quality is a big part of what makes creation so much more advanced than any human invention. There is this know-how that allows you to adapt to almost any situation. It is innate and automatic, but also on some subconscious level, a choice.Loving kindness, compassion, and support is an adaptive choice built on millions of years of evolution that helps us be the best versions of ourselves. The fact that our bodies always make this choice, even if we never think about it, is what helps us survive and thrive

What it also means is that we all have an unlimited amount of metta (i.e., compassion and kindness) available to us in every moment. Our goal with this massage is to tap into what is already such a fundamental part of what we are and help bring it out into the world. What better place to start than to share metta and loving touch with the people who mean the most to us?

As such, at the heart of this massage is the physical application of loving kindness. When you practice on people who you care about and consider some of the reasons why you care about them, these feelings will come pouring out of you. This massage is a life-changing experience because you cannot help but want to live with these positive feelings all of the time.

It starts with this massage, but it can also impact every part of your life. When metta or compassion is at the heart of how you massage, then the session cannot help but go right, and everything you do in the massage becomes an expression of being more and more right with every technique and moment of quality touch.

Once again, tapping into this quality is all about paying attention. The energy of metta is the energy of the present moment. When you pay attention to your breath and immerse yourself into what you are doing, the energy of metta will be there—naturally, effortlessly, and with total abundance.

Transferring this into your massage, the first thing to think of when you begin is happiness. If both you and your partner want happiness, this means that both of you are the same. Every session begins by putting your hands together at your heart. Make that first step a wish for interconnected happiness for both you and your partner.

Visualize love and kindness coming through your palms. As your massage begins, allow your hands to exude this energy and let this feeling be contagious. With every touch, no matter what part of your body makes contact, keep paying attention or trying to pay attention. Within this effort, there is the quality of loving kindness, peace, safety, comfort, respect, and deep wishes of contentment. From there, be aware that what we are doing next is turning metta or loving kindness into a powerful system to give a mutually beneficial massage. With a little practice in getting to know the system, you will know just what to do. The benefits for both you and your partner will surprise and delight you both.

The Second Pillar: Stances

When bringing mindfulness or meditation and metta into your practice, the first priority is to take good care of yourself. The better you feel, the more you will be able to help your partner and practice at the highest level. Furthermore, the more that you are aware of yourself in space, as well as in relation to the working area and your partner, the more you will develop intuitive answers for how to position your body at all times. The first key to this application of having outstanding body mechanics is the effective use of stances. Stances are the positions in which you put yourself when giving the massage and moving from one position to the next. You choose the stances that help you use your whole body so that everything comes from your core (i.e., center) and extends outwards to the part of your body making contact with theirs.

A general rule for all stances is to practice with a straight back and to have your shoulders relaxed. In this way, your body is attentive, your muscles are engaged, and you feel at ease. If you are too rigid or relaxed while you practice, this can put undue strain on your joints, back, or legs. The key is to find the right balance so that you practice comfortably and feel a natural flow with every step of your massage.

This massage is designed to be done on a mat on the ground or on a bed. You can choose what is most comfortable for you and your partner. If your partner is unable to be on the ground with ease, then practice on a bed. If you have difficulty being on your knees or bending your knees, then you can stand or sit next to the bed. The descriptions of each technique will help you no matter what surface you choose to practice on.

I) DIAMOND STANCE / OPEN DIAMOND STANCE

Kneel and sit on your heels. Your back is straight, with your eyes looking forward.

OPEN DIAMOND VARIATION:

Open Diamond is similar to Diamond Stance, except with your knees open more widely.

Furthermore, you can elevate your stance to accommodate size differences.

SAFETY NOTE:

If it is difficult to sit on your heels, then tuck a pillow between your feet and bum. This will ease the pressure on your knees and ankles.

II) KNEELING DIAMOND STANCE

Bring the knees slightly together and come up on your knees.

III) WARRIOR STANCE / OPEN WARRIOR STANCE

Raise your left knee up and bring your foot flat on the floor with your leg extended. Do not extend the knee beyond the toes.

Open Warrior Variation:

This is similar to Warrior, but the raised knee is shifted to the side with the hips facing straight ahead.

GLIDING WARRIOR VARIATION:

Gliding Warrior is used to make adjustments in distance between you and your recipient. You can move in Warrior by extending your front leg and then sliding your back leg along the mat.

IV) TAI CHI STANCE

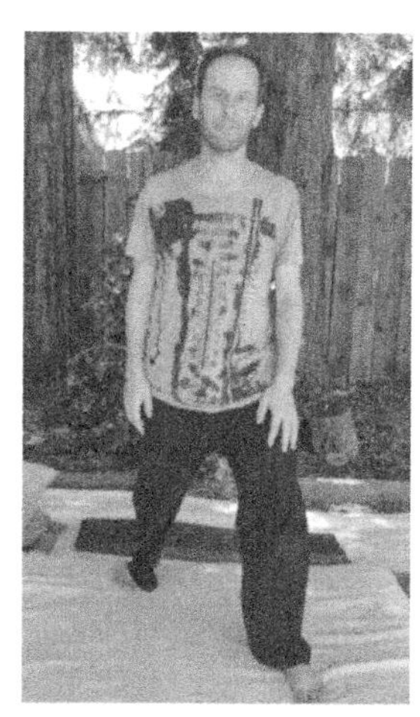

Curl the back toes under, and raise yourself up. With your legs hip-width apart, keep your front leg bent and your back leg straight.

V) HORSE RIDING

Circle one leg out and then the other so that you are in a slight squat. You will use this stance to bend your partner's legs with your legs.

The Third Pillar: Rocking

Rocking is one of the most important aspects of the massage. Rocking helps ensure that you use your whole body with every technique. It is the means by which we alter the pressure and momentum, as well as create leverage during the massage.

When you combine rocking with the correct stance for your body, that helps to ensure that everything you do comes from your core (i.e., the center of your body). This minimizes how much effort it takes to give the massage.

As such, there is a golden rule that is important to internalize as you massage: **"rock first, massage (or touch) second."**

This means that whenever you want to initiate contact, no matter what part of your body makes contact with your partner, you want to ensure that you rock your body first. This is true regardless of whether you are massaging them with your hands, forearms, or feet, or if you are putting them in a guided stretch. Always make sure that you are in a supportive stance, and then rock your body. Thereafter, you will be ready to touch or massage. One other point about rocking is that it also establishes the tempo for the entire massage. The rocking creates a nurturing and relaxing motion that also helps with the flow of the massage.

Your rocking will organically create a deeply relaxing massage experience. There are three rocking techniques, and you can practice these either by sitting in a chair, or more ideally, by positioning yourself in the Open Diamond stance—on a bed, carpet or mat— with your hands on your knees.

I) FORWARD ROCK

Rock your body forward and back, while keeping your back straight and shoulders relaxed. When moving forward, the chin is slightly raised and when moving backward, the chin is slightly tucked to ensure a straight spine.

II) SIDE TO SIDE

Rock your body from side to side like bamboo trees in the wind. The head should follow the spine.

III) WHIRLPOOL ROCK

Spiral your upper body first in one direction, and then make circles in the other direction. Begin slowly and then gradually increase the size of the rotations.

As you do it, try to notice your chin. It should lean forward as you lean forward and tuck in slightly as you lean backwards.

CHAPTER 2: Touch, The Fourth Pillar of Thai Massage

Compassionate touch is at the heart of providing an outstanding massage experience. All contact with your partner is a method of touch. This includes putting your partner into a stretch, working with the energy of the body, and using your hands, arms and feet to provide that incredible feeling of being massaged.

The art of touch is a birth right. It is the dominant sense that we all use when first making sense of our world. From birth until about the age of two, it is far and away the way we relate most to our environment. We used it to help develop a sense of awareness, love, and safety. Once our perception begins to evolve through our eyes and ears, our heightened ability to sense through touch can become lost, but it is not forgotten. To the contrary, because of this primal awareness, it is universal. With the right approach, everyone can tap into that sense and develop the skill to massage at an extremely high level.

The heart of this training is to help you unearth what you already know about touch and develop this sensitivity at the highest level as soon as possible. When learning how to massage, keep in mind that fundamentally there are two things happening concurrently at all times:

1) You are learning how to develop your skill to give a great massage.

2) Your partner is receiving the results of your effort. Accordingly, you want them to feel really good and make sure that they are safe, supported, and can relax even while you are trying to figure this all out.

The good news is that you can achieve both of those objectives with the same common approach. I call it the secret to giving an outstanding massage. It is also how you turn this massage into a moving meditation. **All you need to learn and remember is this one thing: "how slow can you go, how high can you fly?"**

What this means is that the secret to giving an incredible massage, right from the beginning, is to take your time with everything you do. It is to ease into every massage technique and every part of the body that you want to massage.

The more gradual you can be, and the more you take your time and cultivate your listening and noticing skills, the better it will be. You will soar, and you will fly!

The Fourth Pillar: Compassionate Touch

In this book, I will be defining what it means to ease into things, both in a general sense and also in the descriptions of every technique that you will be using.

When you develop an approach that is gradual and measured, you will develop your non-verbal communication skills. With dedicated practice, you will be able to massage as an artisan would be able to mold clay into a most beautiful work of art. You will be able to sense every nuance of a muscle, joint, and tender area of the body, and provide a highly customized way of treating that area and your partner that brings the ideal pressure, perfect stretch, and an unbelievable massage again and again.

At the same time, when you take your time, you are supporting your partner in the best way possible.

You are subtly communicating to your partner that you are proceeding in a careful and supportive way that helps them relax, trust, and let go. The result is that your confidence will build rapidly knowing that you are massaging safely and that your loved ones are enjoying the experience immensely while you fine-tune your craft. Going "slow" can mean several things, which we will define here and subsequently go into much more detail with each specific technique.

Developing "how slow can you go" means:

I) OUTSTANDING COMMUNICATION. THIS INCLUDES:

A. Taking extended time to check in before you begin the massage. If you are helping someone who is new to this, explain how the session will proceed and the parts of the body that you may touch in order to get feedback regarding any areas that your partner would rather you skip.

B. Communicating with your partner during the massage—a lot! Check in for pressure at the start of the massage.

C. Check in for pressure and comfort *anytime you take a calculated risk*. This may include:

  I. A stretch that you think may be beneficial, but you are not entirely certain

  II. Stretching and massaging an area that your partner has explained to be an area of great need

  III. Working an area that you sense is one of great need, even if your partner didn't mention it

IV. When pushing the limits of what you think is ideal pressure

V. When exploring and possibly expanding your partner's edge of flexibility and mobility

VI. Have your partner talk to you as well! The more your partner tells you what they like, the more you are helping each other. Since you will be working on loved ones, they can help you take the mystery out of what it is that they like.

2) HAVE A CLEAR UNDERSTANDING OF HOW MUCH PRESSURE YOUR PARTNER WANTS:

A. Before you begin, ask them on a scale of 1-10 what kind of pressure they want.

B. Test it out by squeezing their forearm or shoulder to ensure that your definition and their definition match.

3) PRACTICE "HOW SLOW CAN YOU GO." SOME OF THE PRIMARY DEFINITIONS INCLUDE:

A. Start with lighter pressure and depth with every technique and proceed to gradually increase things from there:

I. If you know that your partner wants a seven out of ten for pressure, begin each technique at a one or two and gradually increase the pressure. From that starting point, start the communication process before you explore the edge or depth that you think is their max (e.g., when you reach what you think is a five out of ten).

B. When massaging an area, soften it up first and stop at the appropriate level of pressure:

   I. Make circles and explore the area first.

   II. Use lighter pressure before reaching the maximum.

   III. Use alternate palming or soft fists before proceeding with hopping/pressing with both hands or fists at the same time.

   IV. If uncertain regarding the appropriate level of pressure, then check with your partner.

   V. Finding the ideal pressure does not have to mean very deep pressure; in fact, sometimes light is the way to go.

C. When stretching

   I. More repetition and shorter pauses is lighter than one long stretch

4) USE MANY PROPS BOTH FOR THEIR COMFORT AND YOUR OWN. YOU'LL WANT TO HAVE SEVERAL PILLOWS, BLANKETS, AND EVEN TOWELS OF VARIOUS SIZES IF YOU CAN.

As your skill level and comfort level increase, so will your instincts. You will be able to gauge exactly where to stop in a stretch or touch so that it feels good. This is accomplished through awareness, practice, and listening to what your partner is communicating to you. Those answers are all found in the subtle language of non-verbal communication.

However, the ability to massage at the absolute highest level is based on remembering the great habits that you have been practicing since the beginning. When you are comfortable talking to your partner during the massage—even when you already know the answer—then they are an active participant. The power dynamic, and the ability to relax most deeply, rests with your partner. We get to remain humble, respectful, and treat our partner as the amazing individual that they are.

MORE TIPS FOR HOW TO TAKE CARE OF YOUR BODY

- The pressure comes from your center, belly, or core.
    - Whatever part of your body you use, always keep feeling how you can use your whole body to help provide pressure and support yourself in your touch or stretch.
    - Keep your Arms straight, Back straight, and Chin up. These are the "ABCs" of this massage.
    - Do not lock your elbows.
    - Keep bringing attention to your back. Your whole back should be as straight as you can make it, extending from the very top to the bottom.
    - Feel your shoulders relaxed and your neck long.

Massaging With Your Hands

When using your hands, you can use the fleshy part of your palm closest to your wrist, the back of your hand, in between the big knuckles (called soft fists), or your thumbs.

When it comes to giving a massage, your hands are the most vulnerable part of your body and, therefore, the part that is most easily prone to injury. The approaches to protect them are twofold. On the one hand, know how to use them safely. On the other, don't overuse them. Interchange parts of your hands with other parts of your body as massage tools, as needed, so as not to tire out any individual part. What makes giving the massage feel good—while keeping it interesting—is becoming comfortable using all of the parts of your body available to you.

To start this practice round, place a pillow or a folded blanket in front of you. If you are on the ground, sit in kneeling diamond. If you are going to practice on a bed, then put the pillow on the bed and stand comfortably.

PALMS

How to safely use the palm of your hand.

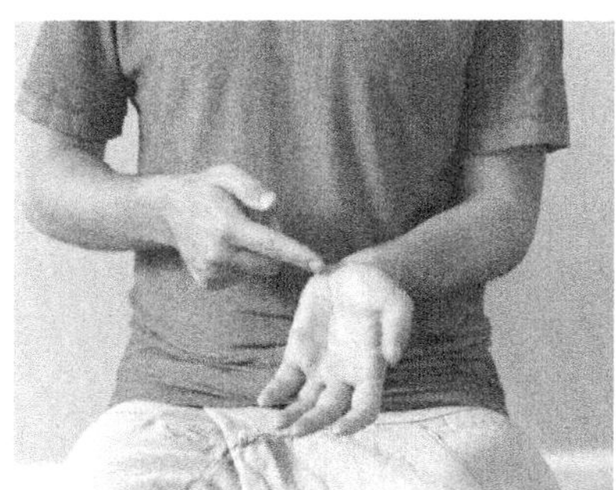

When using your palm, use the part with the most padding, which is close to your wrist. Take a moment to feel your palm and locate that padded part.

From here, do a little test. Put your palm face down and hold your forearm out in front of you so that it is parallel to the ground. Keeping your forearm parallel to the ground, bend your wrist until you feel the first point of resistance.

Figure 1: Wrist Bent 50°

That does not mean bending it as far as you can; rather, it is just to that first point of tension. If you are like me, then that means that you can bend your wrist to approximately 50-60 degrees (Figure 1).

I have yet to meet anyone who can bend their wrist all the way to 90 degrees (Figure 2) without forcing it.

Figure 2: Wrist Bent 90°

Therefore, if you constantly massage with your wrists bent close to 90 degrees, then you are likely to put a fair amount of pressure into your wrists and eventually they will tire of this movement.

You want to be aware of how far forward your shoulders come over your hands when you massage. You can test this by putting your hands on the far end of the pillow, rocking up, and pressing into the pillow. The more forward your shoulders, the more you are bending your wrists. If you want to protect your wrists, simply don't rock as far forward and don't rely solely on your palms when you want to massage with your hands.

The different options available to you when using your palms include:

PALM CHASING PALM

- Rock to one side.
- Apply palm pressure with the equivalent hand.
- Rock to the other side and repeat.

PALM CHASING PALM

- Rock forward.
- Apply palm pressure with both hands simultaneously.
- Protect your wrists (i.e., check the angle of your wrist and avoid angles beyond 80 degrees).

PALM OVER PALM

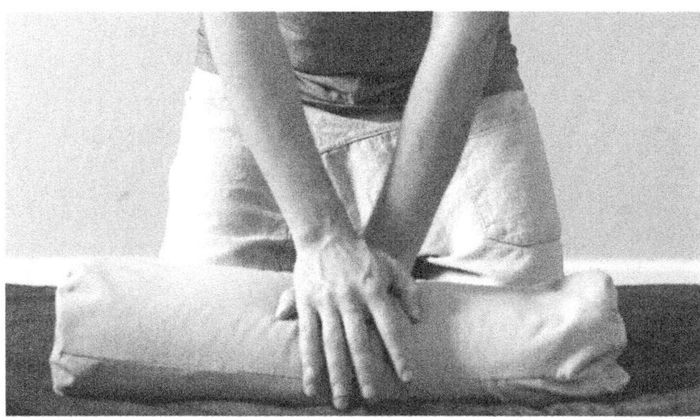

Place one palm over the over to apply pressure. Your bottom hand is comparable to a massage tool that feels for the ideal spot to apply pressure. Once found, keep it relaxed. Your top hand is your power hand. Pressure moves from the center of the body, down the arms, and through the top hand. It is an important palm and wrist-saving technique. You will practice it when massaging the back.

SOFT FISTS

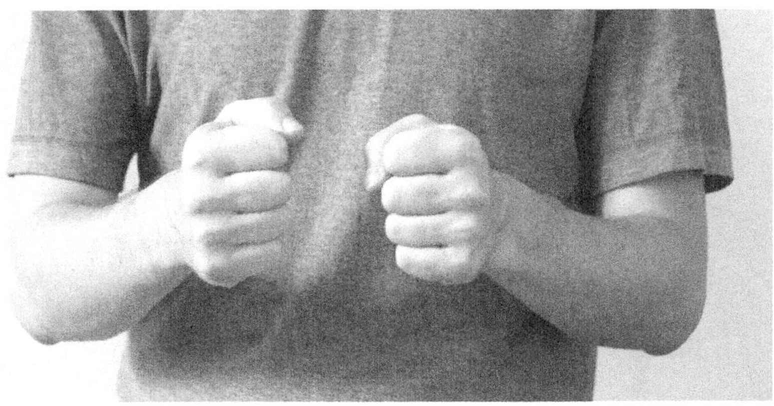

Soft fists are a wonderful alternative to using your palms. You will want to become comfortable massaging with your fists so that you can alternate freely between your palms and fists. This will prove essential when it comes to protecting your hands and wrists.

To use soft fists, make a fist as if you were going to punch someone. That flat area between your knuckles in the middle and the base of your fingers is the area that you will use to massage.
Of course, you will not be punching anyone during this massage, so the idea is to keep your fingers relaxed as you make the fist. Let the energy flow to the tips of your fingers. This is why it's called soft fists.

When you use soft fists, your forearms and wrists will be in a straight line. This means that you will be using entirely different muscles in your hands, wrists, and forearms from palming. Usually, your fists will also be turned out, similar to their position on a steering wheel when driving a car.

FIST CHASING FIST

- Keep your fists and fingers relaxed.
- Rock to one side.
- Apply pressure with the equivalent fist.
- Rock to the other side and repeat.

FIST HOPPING

- Keep your fists and fingers relaxed.
- Rock forward and let your fist make contact with the massage area.
- Your fists are in a straight line with your wrists

THUMBS

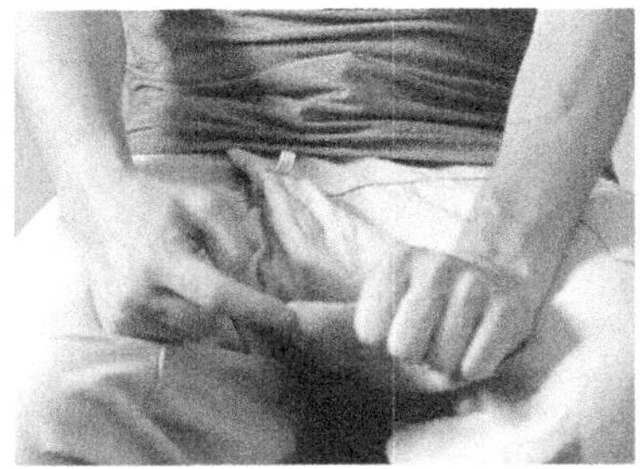

Your thumbs are the most vulnerable part of your body when it comes to massaging, specifically the joint at the base that joins your thumb to the rest of your hand.

That is why, in general, I discourage using your thumbs independently of each other when giving the massage, especially in combination with forward rock, which uses more of your body weight. In this program, we will use the thumbs to help massage the back, and we will use a technique called palm over thumb to help you use your thumbs wisely.

When you do use your thumbs, the part to use is the most padded part, approximately halfway between the tip of your thumb and center line. Take a moment to locate and feel the most padded part of your thumb. When using your thumb, keep it relaxed and relatively close to the rest of your hand, at about a 30-40-degree angle. The farther your thumb is from your hand, the greater the potential to put a lot of pressure on the base.

PALM OVER THUMB

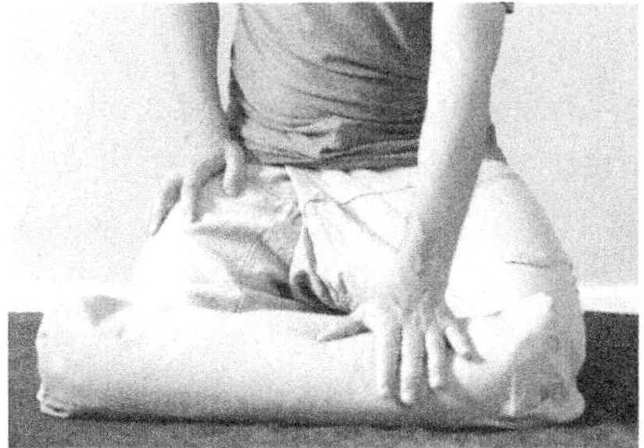

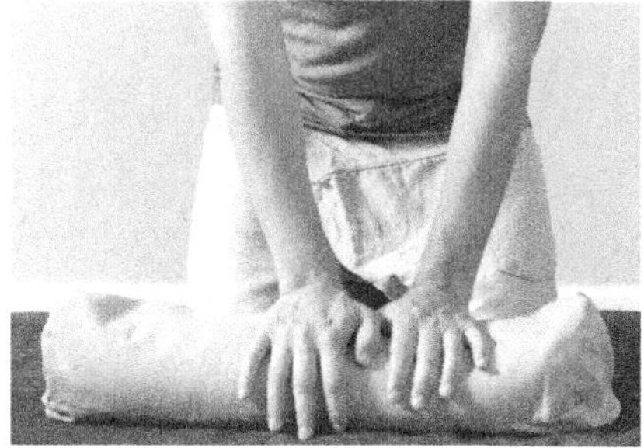

- Place your thumb so that it sticks out from the hand at about a 30-degree angle.
- Place your palm over your thumb.
- Your bottom hand is like a massage tool that feels for the ideal spot to apply pressure. Once found, keep it relaxed.
- Your top hand is your power hand.
- Pressure moves from the center of the body and down the arms and comes through the top hand.
- It is an important thumb-saving technique.

Putting It All Together & Practicing "How Slow Can You Go, How High Can You Fly"

Your first massage is going to be to a pillow or blanket, which works so hard taking care of you when you sleep. The pillow never complains, but it sure can use a good massage! Imagine that your pillow would like an eight out of ten for pressure, and you did a pressure test so you know what that feels like.

If you are on a mat or bed, position yourself in Open Diamond. If you are next to the bed, then stand comfortably. In both cases, feel your back straight, neck long, and shoulders relaxed.

- Place your hands over the far edge of the pillow.
- Start with gentle circles or back-and-forth motions (a one out of ten for pressure.)
- Continue with palm chasing palm: lean to one side with a three for pressure, gradually sink in, and pause for one or two seconds.
- Lean to the next side and repeat.
- Come back to the first side and pause for three or four seconds. Increase the pressure to a five just by pausing and using your natural body weight to increase the pressure.
- Repeat on the second side.
- Make gentle circles to prepare the pillow for deeper pressure.

- Practice palm hopping. Rock up to kneeling diamond, gradually sink in, and pause for one or two seconds (i.e., which increases the pressure to a six) and then gradually ease out.
- Repeat palm hopping—or switch to fist hopping—and pause for five seconds, using your body weight to increase the pressure to an eight.
- Complete the massage by sweeping.
- Repeat the same sequence using fist chasing fist and fist hopping

This exercise is designed to show you the ways to walk up the ladder to gradually increase the pressure and deepen the massage. However, keep in mind that there are many variations within this framework. You will learn how to vary your approach depending on your partner's needs. Now that you have practiced on a pillow, you are just about ready to practice on your partner.

CHAPTER 3: Things to Consider Before, During & After the Massage

In the previous chapter, I mentioned that your partner is your greatest teacher. I also mentioned that the secret to giving an outstanding massage is to internalize "how slow can you go, how high can you fly" with everything you give in this massage.

My wish for you is that this massage helps foster love, connection, and support for you both. At the same time, you get to learn a powerful modality that helps heal, releases tension and stress, and facilitates letting go, relaxation, and revitalization for the body.

Putting that into practice means treating your partner as your primary teacher. As such, it is important to help put them at ease. The best way to accomplish that is to apply the principles of easing in and mindful communication.

It is important to understand what a big thing it can be to ask someone—even if (perhaps especially if) it is your partner for the past 20 years or more—to give up control of their body.
For many people, learning how to receive a massage in a way in which they can relax deeply is as much of a learned skill as giving the massage.

Even if you are massaging someone who can let go easily, the principles of how to make this an incredibly nurturing, caring, and supportive experience remain the same.

It is really very simple because what I am encouraging you to do is talk to your partner and encourage them to talk to you. In general, the more you talk and ask how they are feeling, or explain what you are feeling, the more that they will be put at ease.

The more that they tell you what they are feeling, the faster you will learn how to give them the best massage possible.

What you want to communicate is that you are really listening to their body, their needs, and their wants. You are doing so without judgement. In fact, you are doing this to help and so that you can exchange metta, love, and compassion.

Your massage starts with the very first conversation, so it is important to take some time to consider what you may want to communicate from start to finish. Here are some things to consider:

BEFORE YOUR MASSAGE

- Provide a two or three-sentence description of what this massage is all about. If you are learning this with your life partner, this will not be necessary. However, if you are going to give this to other members of your inner circle, then you will want to be able to describe what this is all about and speak their language. How might you describe this to someone who practices a lot of yoga and does a lot of exercise? How might you describe it to someone who is very stiff?

- What do they need to have on hand in order for this to be a supportive massage experience?

    - Will you do this on a bed or on the ground?

    - What props will you have? That includes pillows, blankets, rolled-up towels, tissues, bolsters, etc.

- The scent of the space
    - Sometimes burning incense or lighting scented candles is exactly what's needed.
    - Sometimes a scent-free space is what's needed.
- Make sure that you are clean and fresh. If you are doing this at the end of the workday, then taking the time to shower so that you are clean—but also to wash that part of your day away—is a great way to get started.
- What will they wear? What will you wear? Usually, this is done wearing comfortable clothing, but what that means is totally up to both of you.
- What kind of music will you play? Choosing a playlist together can be a fun thing to do to help get you started.

DURING YOUR MASSAGE

- Observe their dress, mannerisms, and speech to help get a read on the language you need to speak to your partner.
- Take the time during your first session to have a detailed check-in. At the very least, you will want to ask at least three questions before you begin:
    1. How are you?
    2. Physically, is there anything I should know? Are there any new or old injuries to be aware of?
    3. On a scale of 1-10, what kind of pressure do you like?

- Have a few follow-up questions about their body, even if they say that they have no physical issues. Some people need to be reminded that you are there for them, so more information is helpful. That follow-up question could include, "Do you have any old injuries I should know about?" as well as "How is your neck? How are your shoulders?"

- For any problem areas, ask them to demonstrate their mobility. For example, for neck issues, ask them to look right and left and make half circles. For lower-back issues, perhaps ask them to twist, turn, and lean forward and back.

- Provide a brief overview of the parts of the body that you will work on with the reminder that if there are any areas that they would like you to skip, they can tell you now or during the massage. For example, the face and hair are all areas that some people may not want you to touch, and this is a way to bring it up without drawing attention to any particular area.

- Discuss pressure on a scale of 1-10 and conduct a brief pressure test to gauge that your definition of light, medium, and deep matches theirs by squeezing their forearm.

- Get a sense of their relationship to pain. A massage that works out knots and/or involves stretching is often about exploring the edge of mobility, flexibility, and pressure to work out tension and range of motion. If that is the approach that you are taking, then your partner needs to have a positive relationship to "delicious pain."

- That is, they need to feel as though a little gradual pain is a good thing and, most importantly, that they can breathe comfortably even if it hurts a little. Not all massages must be experienced this way to be effective. This is an energetic massage that needs to be experienced as something positive in order for the body to release all of its natural ability to help itself. A lighter massage can be even more effective than a deep massage when healing is your approach and intention. If your partner is very sensitive to pain and discomfort, then keep things very light and easy, stay away from their pain thresholds, and make sure that there is plenty of communication.

- When it comes to communication and "how slow can you go," you begin by applying a light amount of pressure. Well before you reach what you perceive is their threshold, ask them how it is feeling and if they would like more or less pressure.

  - Ask a closed-ended question when learning how the massage is being received. Asking, "How does this feel?" is an open-ended question and can leave things open to interpretation. Instead, ask if they want more pressure. This will illicit a "yes" or "no" response, which will tell you exactly what you need to know.

  - Ask how things are feeling whenever you are in doubt about how it might be feeling, as well as whenever you take a calculated risk during the massage.

- A calculated risk could include increasing the pressure or depth of a stretch to their limit or just a fraction beyond what you perceive is their upper limit for pressure. It could involve massaging an area that they told you has a lot of pain or tension. It could also involve massaging an area that they did not tell you about, but which you perceive has issues that must be worked out.

- A knot is a bundle of muscle tissue that has tensed up and does not release. It can feel like a small ball or a bigger ball, and it can feel crunchy when you apply pressure or not. They can be the result of overuse, postural issues, lack of use, etc. When it comes to communication and "how slow can you go," you begin by applying a light amount of pressure. Well before you reach what you perceive is their threshold, ask them how it is feeling and if they would like more or less pressure.

  - The way to massage a knot is exactly what we have been talking about already, but with even more care.

  - Ease in with very light pressure and ask how it feels. Gradually increase the pressure if that is what they would like and/or what you sense is needed and continue to check in as needed.

  - Ease off and repeat on the same spot and in areas within close proximity to the first knot.

- The more gradual you can be, the better. You do not need to massage until you feel the knot go away. The fact that you have massaged it will help more circulation and awareness come to the area. Their body will heal and repair itself from there.

- If it is a knot that has been there for a long time, you may be bringing temporary relief and it becomes a regular focus of your massages. In other cases, your massage may help release the knot completely.

- Invite them to let you know what they want. For example, when massaging shoulders, there are often many points of tension and different amounts of pressure that feel good. If they can coach you on what they are feeling and you can take that to heart and adjust what you are doing to meet those needs, then everybody wins.

- Make it a habit to check in for pressure and comfort regularly: at the start, when they turn over, when massaging and stretching areas that push limits, and especially when massaging areas that require greater attention.

- Use many props such as pillows, towels, and blankets. This is for their comfort and your comfort.

AFTER THE MASSAGE

- Show your appreciation for them. This can include things such as hugs, kisses, or giving space.
- Offer your partner a drink of water or tea.
- Encourage calming or intimate activities that you may want to do together, such as taking a bath, enjoying a healthy meal, going for a walk, or making love.
- Remind your partner that some soreness could be expected afterwards if the massage was experienced as particularly deep.
- Drink more than regular amounts of water for 24 hours to help the body flush toxins and return to a healthier state.

Setting Up Your Space

Here are some things that you will need for you and your partner to be comfortable:

ON THE GROUND

- A mat, mattress, or equivalent. In our videos, we use a mat designed for giving massages on the ground. You may contact us to purchase one or visit www.stilllightcenter.com/shop.

    - You can otherwise put a futon or bed mattress on the ground.

    - You can pile up several blankets—we recommend at least four or five—and put yoga mats underneath to give extra cushion for your knees.

    - It is best to put your mat or equivalent on a carpet if you have one available.

- Soft knee pads such as volleyball knee pads are a good idea if you don't have a mat or mattress to practice on.

- Blankets or pillows and towels of varying sizes

    - Soft knee pads such as volleyball knee pads are a good idea if you don't have a mat or mattress to practice on.

    - Blankets or pillows and towels of varying sizes

- Bolsters or rolled-up towels as a face cradle. We sell buckwheat bolsters to support the head and shoulders when your partner is lying face down. They can be purchased on our website www.stillightcenter.com/shop. You can also substitute the bolsters with rolled-up towels or blankets.

- Tissues

- Some awesome music (i.e., whatever will help you and your partner relax)

ON A BED

- Space to walk around the bed is helpful if you will be standing while you give the massage

- A solid chair to sit on for the side lying massage if there is not room to sit on the bed

- Blankets or pillows and towels of varying sizes

  - Blankets may be used to cover your partner if she/he becomes cold.

  - Blankets and pillows are also used to support your partner and help them find optimal comfort.

- Bolsters or rolled-up towels as a face cradle. We sell buckwheat bolsters to support the head and shoulders when your partner is lying face down. They can be purchased on our website www.stillightcenter.com/shop. You can also substitute the bolsters with rolled-up towels or blankets.

- Tissues

- Some awesome music (i.e., whatever will help you and your partner relax)

CHAPTER 4: Creating a Romantic Massage

The massage you are learning here can be used for a multitude of therapeutic reasons. If your partner has aches and pains in their body, be it shoulder issues, neck issues, back problems, headaches, tight hamstrings, tired feet, anxiety, sleep issues and a whole lot more, then chances are they will benefit greatly from this massage.

At the same time, if you want to exchange this massage with your romantic partner, there are a variety of ways you can adapt and adopt these techniques to enhance your relationship.

There are two sides we'll consider here. The first is to massage to help enhance romance and/or love making. The second is working with this massage and its core principals as a way to express love and foster more love in your relationship. As you'll soon see, the two subjects can easily overlap.

Let's start by examining how to adapt this massage to help spice up love making.

If you and your partner want to turn this massage into a sensual massage experience there are a few aspects to consider.

The first is the mood of the massage space. Consider having music, scents and other props, such as silky or soft pillows and blankets that all lend themselves to romance.

What you wear -or don't wear is also something to consider as part of your massage.

This massage can be done on both a mattress on the ground or on a bed. Both the written and virtual course include tips for how to modify the massage when on a bed. If you anticipate the massage leading to love making, then the location of your massage is something to consider. For many, that would mean massaging on a bed.

HOW TO USE OILS WITH THIS MASSAGE

There are many oils on the market you can explore when it comes to giving massage. Massage oils and their various scents specifically made for romantic massage is a multi-million-dollar industry.

Oils serve a dual purpose. They help to soften tight muscles and areas of the body. They also help to accentuate the sensation of touch.

But if you are just starting out with oils and want to keep it simple, two of the very best kinds to use for Thai Massage include either coconut oil or shea butter. To use these oils, spend a moment to soften them in your hands and then apply them to the area you're about to massage.

I like to use those kinds in particular because they are emollient, but not too greasy. In this massage, where you use your forearms and elbows a lot and your hands as seldom as possible, you don't want the skin to be too slippery. Many of the techniques shared in this massage lends itself well to oils, but there are likely some exceptions. At the top of the list would be the Double Leg Massage. That portion of the massage involves stretching and lifting the legs.

I like to use those kinds in particular because they are emollient, but not too greasy. In this massage, where you use your forearms and elbows a lot and your hands as seldom as possible, you don't want the skin to be too slippery.

Many of the techniques shared in this massage lends itself well to oils, but there are likely some exceptions. At the top of the list would be the Double Leg Massage. That portion of the massage involves stretching and lifting the legs.

The way the massage is laid out in this book and virtual course, the Double Leg Massage comes after both the Side Lying and Back Massage. For safety reasons, if you are using oils you may want to consider changing the order and starting with the Double Leg Massage. Once that part is complete, then continue with oils for the other three sections.

If you decide to incorporate the Double Leg portion after you've already used oils, best to take a moment to wipe your hands with a towel to remove any excess. From there, wipe any parts of their body that you would touch with their legs elevated, such as their feet and ankle area. Otherwise, giving the massage remains essentially the same. Start with a little bit of oil and then take your time to soften the area. The easiest places to use oils are where the skin is exposed. The feet, neck and top of the shoulders are at the top of the list. If you also want to use oils on the back, or the legs, then in all likelihood, your partner would remove their clothing for the effected areas before starting the massage.

You may want to have a sheet and blanket to cover them, in case they get cold. In that case, you would uncover the areas you're massaging and keep the rest of the body covered.

It may take a little bit of practice to get the hang of it, but you can use the same guiding principle of "how slow can you go, how high can you fly" to help lead the way. Start with light, but consistent pressure and gradually increase from there. Wait for muscles to soften and melt before applying deeper pressure.

FOCUS ON QUALITY, NOT QUANTITY

I can't emphasize enough how important taking your time is in creating a quality and loving experience.

The less in a rush you are, the more you take the time to experience every touch, their body and the muscles you're making contact with the better. Slowing down to fully appreciate the moment and your partner is what helps to set the mood in the direction of love and love making. If you are using oils, take the time to enjoy the feeling of applying the oils to their skin. Let your fingers slide on and over the muscles, rock gently, make small circles and melt into the moment.

From there, continue with the same approach no matter what part of the body you're using to apply pressure. Feel the warmth of their skin, gently rock your way back and forth with your body onto the area you're massaging and keep finding opportunities to pause and hold delightful pressure. Taking your time is the best way to help them feel good and help you to appreciate the pleasure of quality, loving touch.

WHAT PART OF THE MASSAGE TO FOCUS ON.

Many among us have areas of our body that we prefer to be touched more than others. If for example your partner loves having their back or shoulders touched, then it would make a lot of sense to spend even more time massaging those areas.

As you'll soon learn, the massage includes techniques with your partner lying on their front, their back and their side. If you want to customize the massage to focus on the shoulders and upper back, you could massage their shoulders in all three positions. The neck is a favorite for many people. If that's the case for your partner, then consider giving an extended neck massage, especially towards the end of your treatment once they are in a heightened state of relaxation.

If you only have a few minutes, you might want to consider making your entire massage the sweet ending portion of the treatment which focuses exclusively on the neck, head and top of the shoulders. From there, as you complete your session, you could lean in for a kiss, a hug and continue on. To help find out where your partner prefers to be touched, take time at the beginning to check in with your partner. Ask them where they would like to be touched more, where they might like to be touched less and make choices from there. Invite them to keep letting you know what they like throughout the massage.

RELEASE EXPECTATIONS, FOCUS ON INTENTIONS

Making a massage part of your date night, does not have to mean that you will make love. In fact, so often, it is the expectations we set of how the date should go and what the massage should be that can get in the way of the best experience possible.

Your mindset is such a vital component to having a romantic experience. In just about every situation in our lives, there is the part we're in control of and the part we're not. Putting our attention on the parts we are not in control over -such as getting you and/or your partner "in the mood" is often an invitation for disappointment. As such, it is important to release the outcome.

Where should your focus be instead when giving this massage? That's what intentions are all about. That is how you set the space. Before you begin your massage, that could include having in your mind a desire to please your partner and show them how much you love and care for them and to do it in a way that feels so pleasurable for you as well.

While you are massaging, you can return to that intention regularly.

When you are able to get fully engaged in what you're doing, the quality of the experience has room to grow. Your hands, your elbows, your body will be more in alignment with the moment and with your partner. The quality of touch will be impacted, your presence, the love that is being shared all have more room to flourish.

To help amplify the love, the mood, the experience, my best advice is keep coming back to your intentions, your love for your partner, finding joy in the experience, feeling good in your body, helping to ensure they feel loved, supported and heard in theirs. The more that becomes your focus, the better the experience and the more natural a transition to love making as a further outcome of the experience.

But even if love making does not become an extension of the massage, don't let that define the experience. Any opportunity to share deep connection, to come together, to be open to each other and what might come next is so valuable. And what it might lead to, whether in the moment or in the future might be better than any expectations you had going into the session.

Where should your focus be instead when giving this massage? That's what intentions are all about. That is how you set the space. Before you begin your massage, that could include having in your mind a desire to please your partner and show them how much you love and care for them and to do it in a way that feels so pleasurable for you as well.

While you are massaging, you can return to that intention regularly.

When you are able to get fully engaged in what you're doing, the quality of the experience has room to grow. Your hands, your elbows, your body will be more in alignment with the moment and with your partner.

The quality of touch will be impacted, your presence, the love that is being shared all have more room to flourish.

To help amplify the love, the mood, the experience, my best advice is keep coming back to your intentions, your love for your partner, finding joy in the experience, feeling good in your body, helping to ensure they feel loved, supported and heard in theirs. The more that becomes your focus, the better the experience and the more natural a transition to love making as a further outcome of the experience.

But even if love making does not become an extension of the massage, don't let that define the experience. Any opportunity to share deep connection, to come together, to be open to each other and what might come next is so valuable. And what it might lead to, whether in the moment or in the future might be better than any expectations you had going into the session.

THAI MASSAGE AND LOVE

That leads me to how this massage can be part of not only a romantic exchange, but an enhanced relationship that is more loving with each passing day.

I have taught Couples Thai Massage to people at all stages in their relationships. But one story that stands out is of a couple who had been together for almost 30 years and had raised several kids together.

They came to the workshop so that they could rekindle their love for each other.

They also came to the workshop with the baggage that can accumulate when you've been with someone for nearly three decades. At first, some of those challenging inter-personal dynamics, such as getting on each other's nerves came to the surface. But over the course of the weekend, all of that began to melt. They softened in each other's presence.

Those habits and patterns that had defined a lot of their dynamics started to fade away, and in its place came a deep love and appreciation for each other. And with it came immense gratitude for what the massage and these methods had offered them. They had found each other and the deep love they shared. The million dollar question I'm sure that you're asking is how did they do it? And how can you and your partner do it as well? I want to preface this part by first saying that you don't need to be in a challenging place with your partner in order to fall more in love with them while learning and giving this massage. Quite the contrary!

Where should your focus be instead when giving this massage? That's what intentions are all about. That is how you set the space. Before you begin your massage, that could include having in your mind a desire to please your partner and show them how much you love and care for them and to do it in a way that feels so pleasurable for you as well.

While you are massaging, you can return to that intention regularly.

When you are able to get fully engaged in what you're doing, the quality of the experience has room to grow. Your hands, your elbows, your body will be more in alignment with the moment and with your partner.

The quality of touch will be impacted, your presence, the love that is being shared all have more room to flourish.

To help amplify the love, the mood, the experience, my best advice is keep coming back to your intentions, your love for your partner, finding joy in the experience, feeling good in your body, helping to ensure they feel loved, supported and heard in theirs. The more that becomes your focus, the better the experience and the more natural a transition to love making as a further outcome of the experience.

But even if love making does not become an extension of the massage, don't let that define the experience. Any opportunity to share deep connection, to come together, to be open to each other and what might come next is so valuable. And what it might lead to, whether in the moment or in the future might be better than any expectations you had going into the session.

This massage by its very nature, as well as the ways I coach you to work together brings out the best in both of you. It will nurture and foster love in all its glory and all your glory. It will happen organically when you practice with an open mind, heart and body and take it step by step.

As you have already learned, at the heart of this practice are two essential qualities. One is that this massage is love turned into a form. That is the first pillar of the exchange and in my opinion the only prerequisite for giving a great massage. You both will be tapping into this energy, this feeling, these sensations every step of the way. As such, in practical terms, when you are learning and massaging, all you need to do is keep doing your best. Continue to make choices that help you to feel good in your body when you give, work with the core principles of being gradual and communicating well and they will feel good from all the great ways the massage feels.

I would encourage you, especially if you're going through a challenging time to meditate together before starting to massage each other. One defining characteristic of "How slow can you go, how high can you fly" means taking the time to make space for each other, for the love to flow, for you both to be available to it.

It will help make learning the massage and giving it that much more of a pleasure. If you want some guided meditation for love and peace that you can use, check out this link on my YouTube channel to get started. https://youtu.be/4ebHd0akgmo

Because love, kindness and compassion are at the heart of this exchange, you can't help but be affected by it. It will help both of you to soften, to let go of the stresses of the day and your life, even before you start massaging. Begin with that mindset. You are welcoming love, connection and caring into the space and into the exchange that's about to take place.

From there, with every technique you give, you'll continue to invite that in. Welcome that energy, that knowledge, that wisdom into your hands and your body as you massage them and that is what you'll be sharing and exchanging with each other. You'll feel it deeply when you're the giver and they'll feel that quality and that energy as they receive.

The second essential component of this massage, and the way I coach you to learn is to realize just how important the role that healthy communication plays. Communication is at the heart of every relationship and the more you practice it, the better your relationship. That is also true of this massage, both when you're learning it and when you practice it. In fact, I call communication the flip side of "how slow can you go, how high can you fly" Thus, as you are taking your time and being gradual with whatever technique you're giving, take a moment to ask how the massage is feeling.

The best time to check in with your partner is before the pressure or the depth goes too deep. Recognize that when you massage someone, even when it is your long-time partner, it can be a big deal for the receiver to give up control over their body.

You make it better, or easier for them to relax and let go when you talk and when you encourage them to share what they are feeling.

And there are many times in the massage where you take what I call a calculated risk. The risk is not that you might hurt them, but that it could feel uncomfortable, unpleasant, too deep, you name it. That can happen when you massage an area of great need, an area that's been injured, a tight muscle, a stressed-out body and a stressed-out person.

Therefore, a great habit to develop is to ask how they are feeling and if they want any more (or any less) pressure. And ask these questions while the pressure, or the stretch is on the lighter side of what they like. When you massage in this way, then your partner is being heard, respected, appreciated and loved. I'm sure you can start to see that when this is how you approach the massage, that can't help but foster more love between you.

And if you keep doing that over the course of a 1-hour massage, those feelings keep growing and growing. And if you keep massaging each other ever week for the life of your relationship, the quality of love that grows becomes exponentially great. What's more, these newfound communication methods you're sharing in the massage, can also be applied to other parts of your life.

This is exactly what happened with that couple. They invested in listening to each other, to making sure that the receiver was giving advice about what they liked in a clear, but supportive way. They made sure the giver would ask on a regular basis, with an open mind and heart, because they were interested in supporting the other and learning what they like to the best of their ability. So that then becomes the real secret of how giving this massage helps to foster tremendous amounts of love for you both. Treat each other as your number one teacher and as the amazing person that you both are.

If you're the giver, let your partner know that you encourage their feedback. They don't need to wait for you to ask how it's feeling. If there's something they like about the experience, or something they don't, let them know that you would like to hear about it. If there's a great spot on their body that you're massaging, encourage them to share that information.

You in turn as the giver can take that as a cue to spend even more time on that spot and in the surrounding areas. And massage in a way where you're taking your time, you are listening, you are responding with your whole heart and your full awareness. You of course will also ask questions and check in when you're taking those calculated risks and when it's all said and done this massage exchange becomes a transformative experience. You are massaging from an ever-deepening place of love, appreciation and presence.

They are receiving from a place of gratitude, love and joy. Love flows, appreciation for your partner grows and you can both take it from there!

PART 2:

GIVING COUPLES THAI MASSAGE

CHAPTER 5: Side Lying Massage

GETTING SET UP ON THE SIDE

Your partner should be set up lying on their side as comfortable as possible. Typically, this means having one leg bent, the other straight and a pillow under the head thick enough so as to encourage a straight spine

TRANSITION TO SIDE LYING MASSAGE

- Set up blankets, mats, bolsters or pillows at hip level on the left
- Have a thick pillow under your partner's head
- The amount of props to put under their leg or head is dependent on the size of your partner. It is a good idea to have 3 or 4 props to put under the leg and one thick pillow for under their head

PALM PRESS THE ARMS

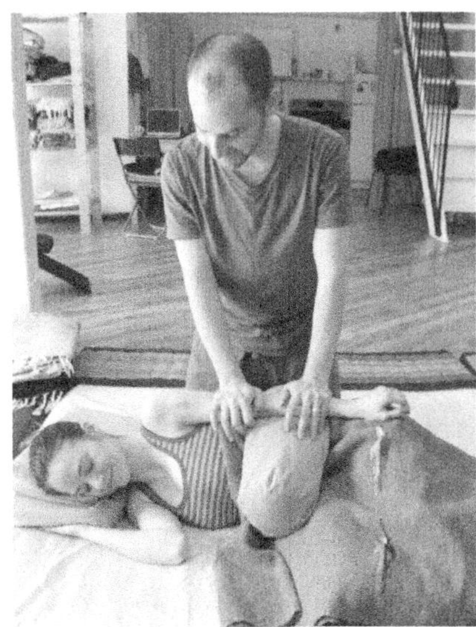

A great way to massage the arm, the side body and to ground your partner

TRANSITION

- Shift into kneeling diamond centered at the elbow
- Your legs should make light contact with the lower back

TECHNIQUE

- Place a pillow or bolster under their arm to close the gap between body and arm
- Place their arm along the side of their body
- Start with palm chasing palm with one hand starting at the wrist and the other just above the elbow

- Continue by palm pressing. Begin on either side of the elbow, palm press the arm with one hand moving toward the shoulder and the other moving towards the wrist
- After two or three repetitions add traction by turning your hands at their wrist and shoulder and press down and away

BENEFITS

- Massage for the arm and particularly beneficial for the joints at the wrist and shoulder
- Relaxes the spine and the ribs
- Helps to encourage deeper breathing

Tips, Precautions, Making this a Universal Technique

FOR THEIR SAFETY AND COMFORT

When massaging a woman it is generally a good idea to put a pillow or bolster in between her body and her arm to close the gap that comes with the natural curve of the body. It is also pretty comfortable for men.

How slow can you go:

- Begin with a light touch and alternate the pressure from one hand to the next
- If your partner likes more pressure increase by adding longer pauses and more pressure
- Add 'palm hopping' or pressing with both hands at the same time

FOR YOUR SAFETY AND COMFORT

Keep your shoulders over your wrists. This will help to ensure you use your body more than your arms or hands to apply the technique. Light contact with your thighs against their body will also help you with balance and leverage

ON A BED:

- This is similar to massaging on a mat
- Just take care to make sure you can keep your balance as you rock from side to side if kneeling on the bed
- Alternatively your partner can be set up close to the edge of the bed and you can stand on the ground for the Side Massage. You may need to stand on a pillow or low stool to give yourself more height depending on your height relationship to your partner

NECK & SHOULDER MASSAGE

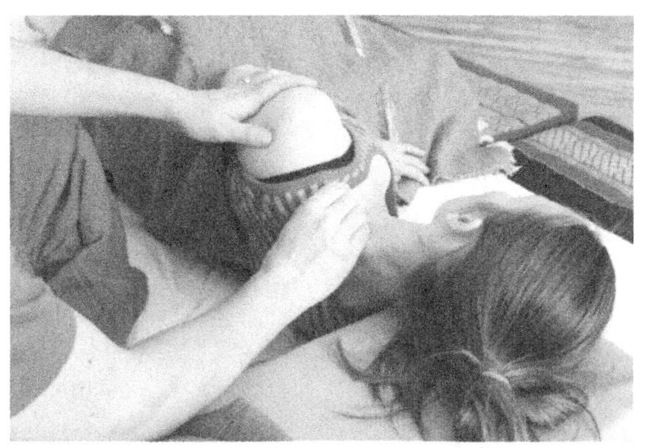

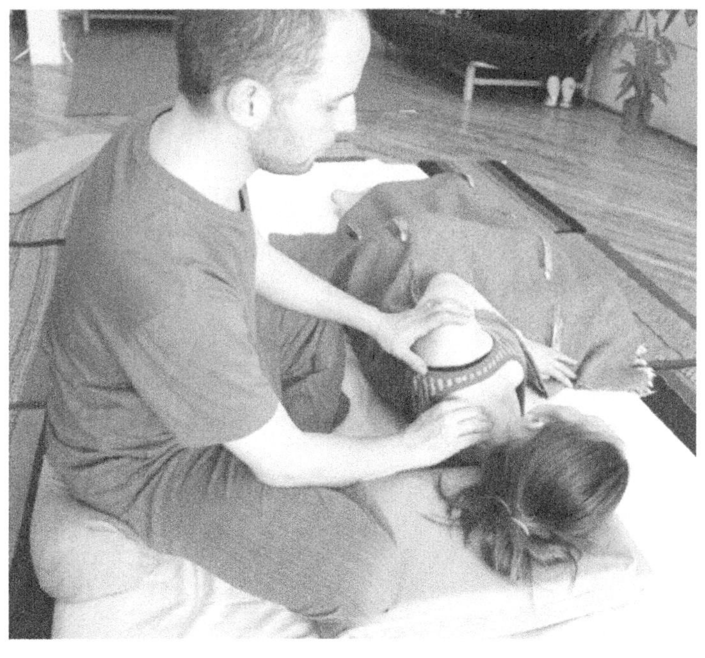

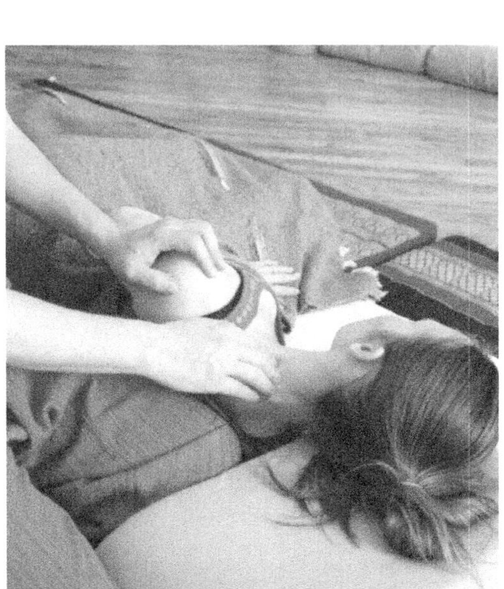

A free-form relaxing massage for the neck and shoulders

TRANSITION

- You can work the neck and shoulders in diamond stance in two positions:
  - In diamond with knees facing the head
  - In diamond turning to face your partner's back
  - Choose the direction(s) that is most comfortable for you
- Alternatively, sit on a pillow instead of sitting in diamond stance

TECHNIQUE

- Free form massage of the neck and shoulders using your fingertips, palms, thumbs, etc.

- Take it nice and slow and spend extra time working any areas that are especially tense

BENEFITS

- Relaxing massage and working out knotted muscles and energy blockages in the neck and shoulders.

Tips, Precautions, Making this a Universal Technique

FOR THEIR SAFETY AND COMFORT

This may be an area that carries a lot of tension and is very sensitive, especially in the neck area so practicing with a light and feathery touch to begin is especially important and get lots of feedback about how it feels.

How slow can you go:

- Start with lighter pressure than your partner asked for

- Circle into the area first with your fingertips for 10-20 seconds then slowly squeeze, massage or add pressure as you see fit

- Check in for pressure to ensure they are comfortable

- Spend extra time massaging sore, stiff or tender areas, but keep it soft

FOR YOUR SAFETY AND COMFORT

It is so important to protect your thumbs and use proper technique and at the same time don't overdo it. Remember! "Rock First, Massage Second"

Be aware of the joint at the base of your thumb and do not overuse it. For especially large and tight partners there is only so much you should do to massage the shoulders with your thumbs. Later in the massage you will use your feet and you will have a second opportunity to massage this area, so no need to overdo it. The neck massage should be soft and help take your partner into deeper relaxation.

ON A BED

- You can try this sitting on a pillow on the bed
- Or you can try sitting on a chair at the edge of the bed and sit on pillows if needed to give yourself added height

BACK PEDAL

Massaging with your feet for a supportive back stretch, back massage and chest opener

TRANSITION

- Bring your partner's arm behind their back while you sit behind them

TECHNIQUE

- Massage up and down the side of the back, under the scapula, the sacrum and lower leg wherever you can apply pressure with your feet.

- You can use both feet to massage up and down one side; or one foot stays on the lower back while the other finds sweet spots to massage including under the shoulder blade; or walk on both sides of the back placing the middle of your foot over the spine so as not to apply pressure;

ON A BED

- Eases tension and massages a majority of the back
- Supportive back bend and chest opener

Tips, Precautions, Making this a Universal Technique

FOR THEIR SAFETY AND COMFORT

This is the first time you are using your feet to give a massage and it is your first stretch. I recommend proceeding with care at a slow pace. Develop what we call a 'feather touch' which means to apply less pressure than your partner asks for so you can develop greater sensitivity on how to massage effectively with your feet for less flexible partners. With partners who are quite stiff or have an injury in their backs and shoulders be careful not to pull back at all on the arm you are holding. The purpose of holding that arm is to keep from kicking your partner forward and out of the side position.

How slow can you go:

- As with any stretch begin with lots of repetition and 1 second pauses
- As their back relaxes increase the pause by 1-5 seconds depending on their flexibility
- The longer you keep them in this stretch and the longer you press in one place the deeper the stretch becomes

FOR YOUR SAFETY AND COMFORT

Make sure to set yourself up so you are centered behind the back so that it is easy to reach. Your hand that is not holding their hand can be on the mat behind you to help to support yourself. Feel free to change hands if they get tired.

ON A BED

- If you are sitting on a bed it needs to be wide enough to have enough room for you to settle behind them
- Otherwise you can do this sitting on a chair behind your partner, but the chair needs to be solid. Best not to use a folding chair or one that is on wheels in order to do this safely. If you feel the front legs of the chair start to raise as you press with your feet then best to stop and move the chair back before continuing

MASSAGING THE GLUTES

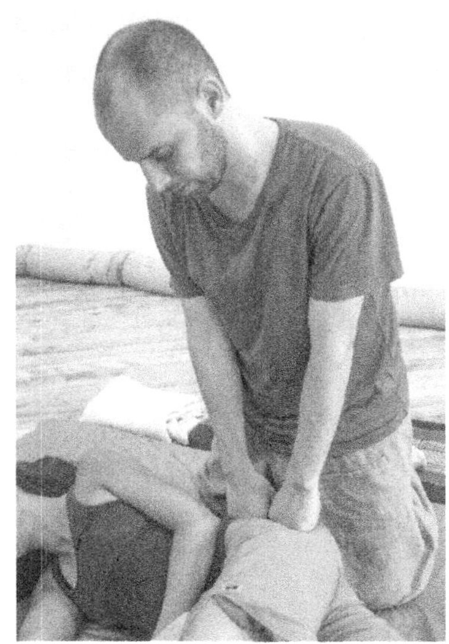

All kinds of heavenly ways to massage those hard to reach and highly used bum muscles

TRANSITION

- Shift up into kneeling diamond facing the glutes

TECHNIQUE

- Massage soft tissue spots all around the bum and close to the hip using soft fist, palm over palm, forearm and elbows

BENEFITS

- Eases sciatic and piriformis issues
- Relaxes the legs and lower back
- Massages a key area where tension accumulates and is hard to relax on their own

Tips, Precautions, Making this a Universal Technique

FOR THEIR SAFETY AND COMFORT

The area right around the hip can be particularly sensitive which is also very effective when you work gradually. If your partner is very sensitive to pain you may want to skip it the first time you massage them until they know what to expect.

How slow can you go:

- Start with lighter pressure than your partner asked for
- Circle into the area first with your palms or fists for 10-20 seconds then slowly press with a rocking motion and add pressure as you see fit
- Check in for pressure to ensure they are comfortable

- Spend extra time massaging sore, stiff or tender areas, but keep it soft

- If you are sitting on a bed it needs to be wide enough to have enough room for you to settle behind them

- Similarly for deep pressure find a deep soft spot, place your elbow and lean into your palm either with your head or your other hand

***Video Tip*: Head over to my YouTube channel to watch a video of how to do the "Rolling Pin" technique: https://youtu.be/HHBMJv0Y-B0**

FOR YOUR SAFETY AND COMFORT

The key for you is to try to rely on other parts of your body besides your thumbs to do the work. These are some of the deepest and biggest muscles of the body so it is best to rely on other parts of your body to help.

ON A BED

- Take care to keep your balance. It may be easier for you to stick to using your forearms and elbow

- If standing next to the bed keep your shoulders over your hands so that your body helps to apply pressure. This could be a good time to stand on a firm pillow or short stool depending on your height relationship with your partner

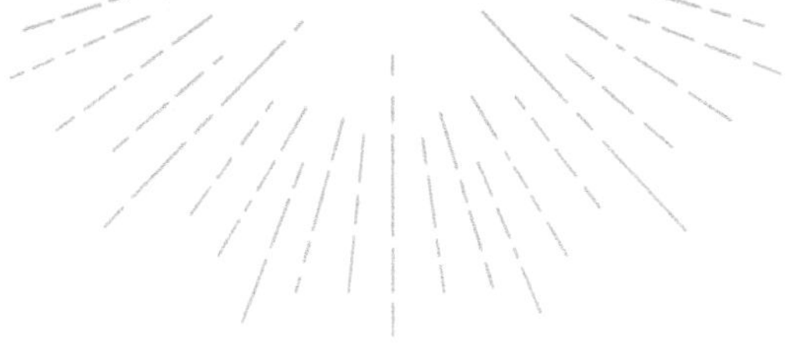

MASSAGING THE ENERGY LINES ON LEGS

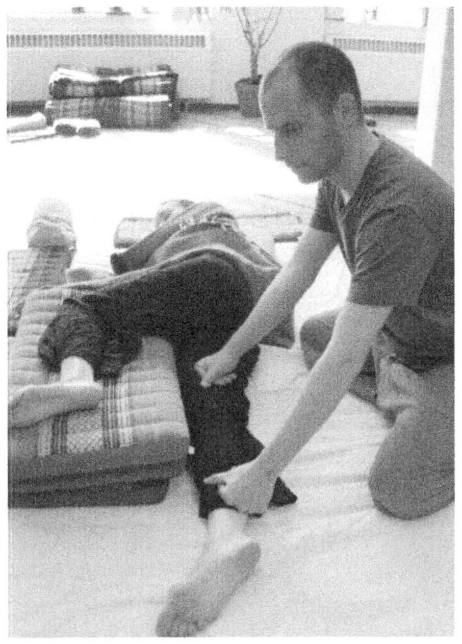

Massaging the energy line (or sen line) works the back of the leg which helps to alleviate lower back issues.

TRANSITION

- Move down the body until you are in an open diamond centered behind the straight leg
- Maintain enough distance so that you keep to the ABCs: Arms are straight, Back is straight and Chin is up

TECHNIQUE

- This energy line runs straight from Achilles tendon over the back of the knee and to the crease where the leg meets the bum

- Massage the energy line in open diamond placing one hand on the Achilles and the other on the back of the knee

- Use fist chasing fist or palm chasing palm with one hand pressing towards the knee while the other presses towards the top of the leg

- Apply pressure with one hand on the Achilles, pause for 1 – 3 seconds, release and then press with your hand that is on the back of the knee. Release and move hands up the leg and repeat

- Time it so one hand reaches the top of the leg while the other reaches the back of the knee and then use fist chasing fist to return to the beginning

- Repeat two more times

BENEFITS

- This energy line is particularly effective at helping to release tension in the legs and in relaxing the back

Tips, Precautions, Making this a Universal Technique

FOR THEIR SAFETY AND COMFORT

Massaging an energy line is all about loving kindness and compassion- metta, so we don't need to use much pressure. The greater benefits will be felt the more you pay attention to your work. In this case it is ok to apply pressure on the back of their knee as long as you keep it light

How slow can you go:

- Keep the pressure light
- Pause for 1-3 seconds with each press

FOR YOUR SAFETY AND COMFORT

The keys to massaging an energy line are to be centered and to face your work. Usually the center of the leg is their knee so use that as a guide. If you are on the bed or mat, use open diamond with your knees as wide as you can in order to support your lower back.

The rhythm is like a walking pendulum where you swing to one side, use that same hand to apply pressure for a few seconds and then swing to other side and do it again. Move your hands up or down the leg to the next position and repeat.

ON A BED

- This can be done either in kneeling diamond on the bed or standing with your partner close enough to the edge

- If you are on the tall side and standing then best to move back far enough to maintain a straight back

Massaging the energy or sen lines

The word 'sen' refers to the vital energy said to run throughout various channels, meridians or lines in our body. Every Eastern approach to wellness and understanding of the body works with this fundamental knowledge towards building a healing modality. In yoga we refer to encouraging the flow of prana in the nadis and in Chinese medicine we talk about chi and meridians. Fundamentally our approach to touch has its roots in Thai Massage and it is all about working with a person's energy. Putting people in stretches, using a multitude of touch techniques, focusing on the energy lines and customizing the experience towards different qualities of touch are how we touch in a most intelligent way that honors all the wonderful abilities and complexities of our partner.

We want to treat the energy, encourage its healthy movements, release blockages and facilitate the body's natural ability to help and reset itself. When working the energy lines I always try to remind my students to create a relationship with energy. Your intention is much more important than the exact running of the lines. By starting with light touch and seeing the results you'll develop greater sensitivity and come to realize just how powerful your results can be with minimal effort.

There are different approaches when it comes to choosing which side of the body to start with. In practice for a general massage, I often choose to start on the side that is in better shape. It gives us a way to learn what the body feels like before proceeding onto the side that requires greater care and caution.

It also allows our partners to experience and associate the massage as a pleasant one before working on more sensitive areas. That can help reinforce the notion that the massage feels good and is helpful, making it easier for them to relax, release and let go in areas where the first reaction may otherwise be to resist, tense up and hold on.

All in all my recommendation is to do what comes most naturally to you and remember that the first basic of meditation and metta will guide you. Listen to your intuition, practice with loving kindness and compassion and know that everyone's right when metta is where your massage comes from.

TRANSITIONING TO THE NEXT PARTS OF THE MASSAGE

When you finish the first side, ask your partner to turn to the other side as you adjust the pillows.

When you finish the second side, ask your partner to turn face down to get ready for the back massage.

Help to make them comfortable for the back massage by placing bolsters or rolled up towels under their head. Have a pillow handy to put under their abdomen if necessary if they experience any back pain while lying face down.

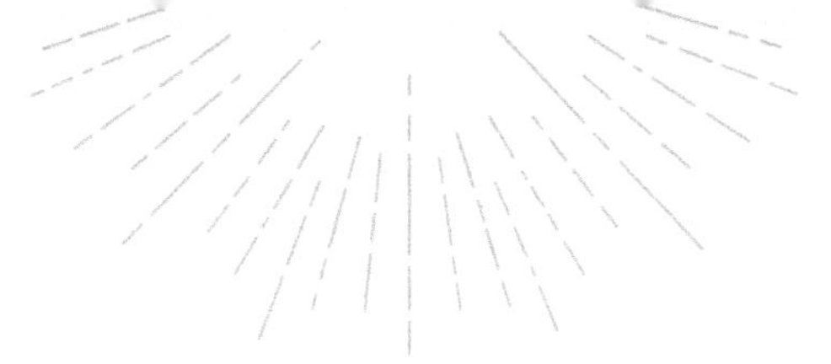

SOLE ROLL

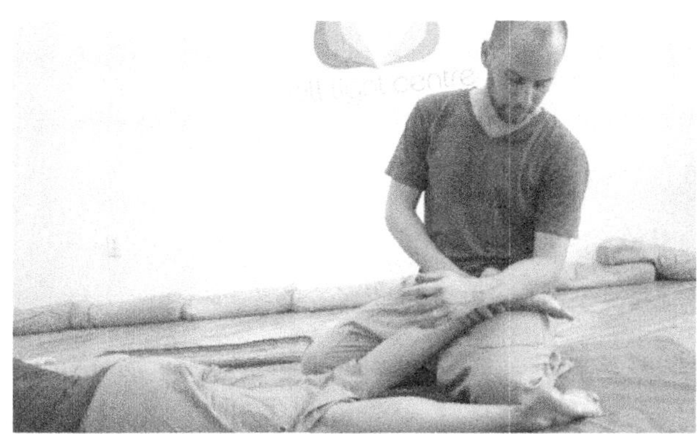

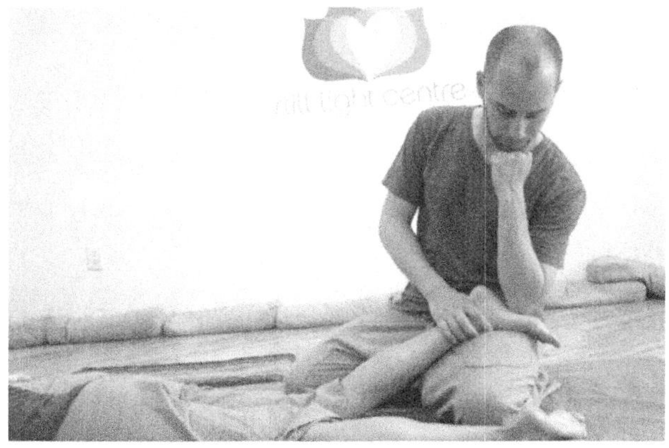

Use your forearm and elbow to give a great foot massage

TRANSITION

- Adjust their feet so that the big toes point to each other and there is about a fist or foot width of distance between them.

- Sit in an open diamond, place a pillow on your lap and then have their foot rest over your outside thigh (if you're massaging their right foot it'll be over your left thigh)

TECHNIQUE

- Adjust their feet so that the big toes point to each other and there is about a fist or foot width of distance between them.
    - Palm faces down
    - Place the center of your forearm under their heel
    - Lean until you have adequate pressure
    - Maintain the pressure and roll until your palm faces up
    - Repeat
    - Use the part closer to your elbow for more precise pressure or to use more pressure
- Use your elbow on the foot to sink into cushy and deeper spots
    - Let your head rest in your head to help apply pressure –and to have fun!

Tips, Precautions, Making this a Universal Technique

FOR THEIR SAFETY AND COMFORT

The entire body is represented on the foot so someone with a lot of tension in the body may also have a lot of tension in the foot. Practicing 'how slow can you go' will be especially important for that partner. Chances are that if your partner is very ticklish they may be very relaxed by this point so they may not be ticklish now. However, if your partner is ticklish using consistent and deeper pressure may be necessary or you may have to skip this part of the session.

How slow can you go:

- Begin with a feather -light- touch and short pauses
- Check with your partner for pressure and make any adjustments
- Slowly and gradually increase the pressure and the pauses, whether using your forearm or elbow
- Repeat on parts of the foot that need extra attention (usually there are great spots to find in the middle of the foot and close to the heel)

***Video Tip*: Head over to my YouTube channel to watch a video of how to do the "Rolling Pin" technique: https://youtu.be/HHBMJv0Y-B0**

FOR YOUR SAFETY AND COMFORT

There are so many wonderful spots you can find when working with your forearm and elbow. Our goal is to develop the same sensitivity in using our forearm and elbow as we would with our hands. As you make contact with the forearm try to feel the tissue close to the surface spreading and then slowly sink in to deeper tissue. See what it feels like to shift and turn your forearm or elbow ever so slightly.

More than likely there will be more spots to sink in. If sitting in open diamond is challenging you may want to place a pillow or bolster between your legs to take pressure off your knees and ankles.

You can also sit cross legged on a pillow. As an alternative to rolling pin, you can also try squeezing the foot with your hands and then try using your elbow to sink into spots.

ON A BED

- If it is difficult to find a comfortable way to sit in open diamond you can try softly squeezing the foot with your palms and using your elbow to sink into spots
- Easiest would be to sit on a chair at the foot or on the side of the bed

CALF ROLL

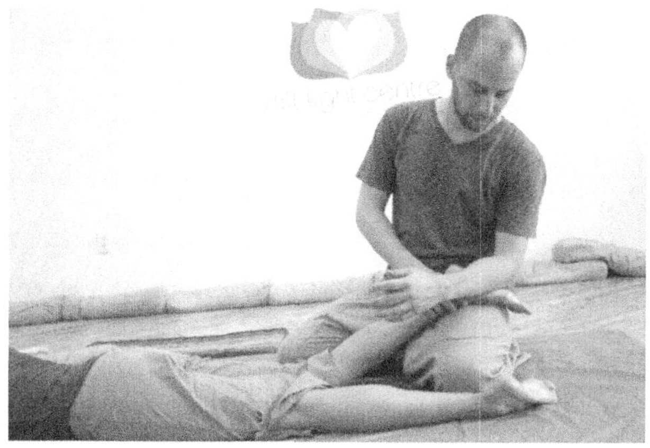

Use your forearm to give a relaxing calf massage

TRANSITION

- From Sole Roll you are already in position for Calf Roll
- Switch the forearms (you can keep the pillow on your lap with their leg resting on the pillow)

TECHNIQUE

- Use the center of your forearm on the calf as a 'rolling pin'
  - Palm faces down
  - Place the center of your forearm under their heel
  - Lean until you have adequate pressure
  - Maintain the pressure and roll until your palm faces up
  - Repeat

ON A BED

- Relaxes the calf which tends to have a profound effect on the whole body

Tips, Precautions, Making this a Universal Technique

FOR THEIR SAFETY AND COMFORT

The calf consists of two muscles and in order for it to feel most comfortable it is best to use the center of your forearm in the middle of their calf. When you roll on the edge of the muscles it can feel pretty intense. A little bit of pressure goes a long way!

How slow can you go:

- Begin with a feather touch and short pauses
- Check with your partner for pressure and make any adjustments
- Slowly and gradually increase the pressure and the pauses
- Repeat on parts of the calf that needs extra attention

FOR YOUR SAFETY AND COMFORT

Check to make sure your shoulders are relaxed, your neck long and your back relaxed. You want to feel at ease as you roll.

An alternative to rolling pin would be to let their leg lit flat and use your hands to softly squeeze the calf. You can also make a soft fist and gently rub the calf.

ON A BED

- If it is difficult to sit in open diamond you can let their leg lie flat and try softly squeezing the calf with your hands
- Easiest would be to sit on a chair at the foot or on the side of the bed

THE FROG

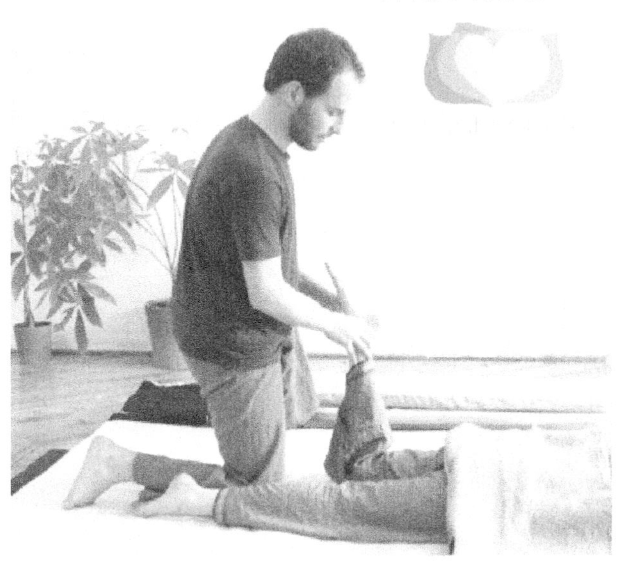

TRANSITIONING INTO THE FROG

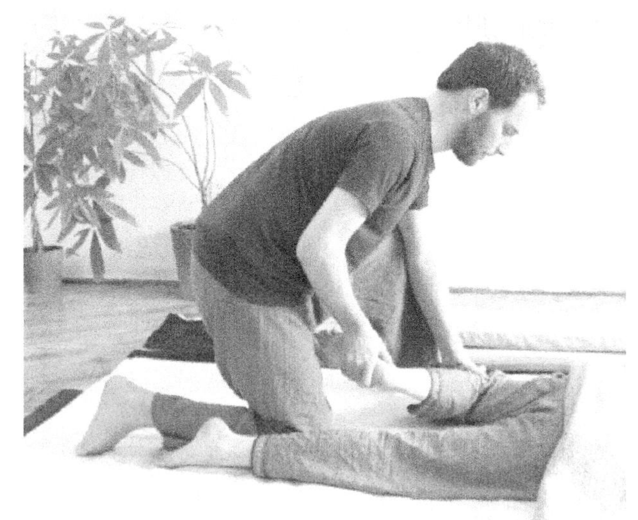

STEP 1: 3 WAYS TO MASSAGE THE CALF DEPENDING ON YOUR SIZE RELATIONSHIP AND COMFORT

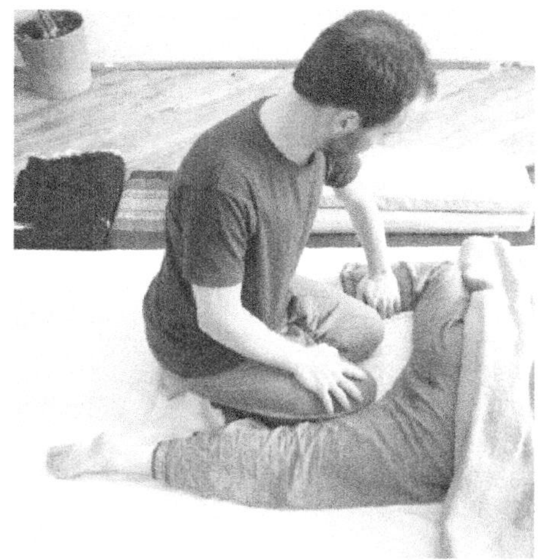

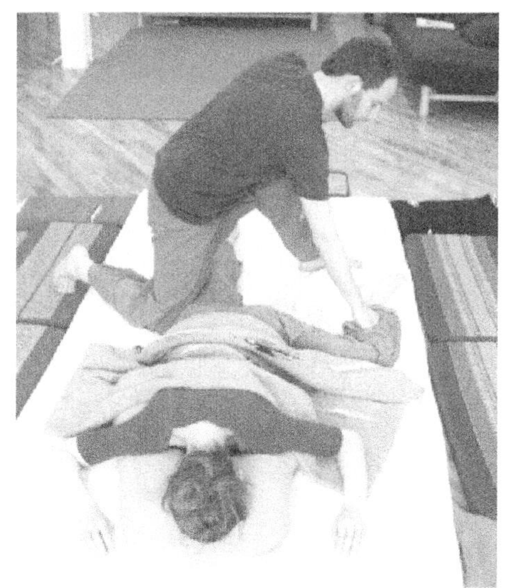

STEP 2: MASSAGING THE HAMSTRINGS

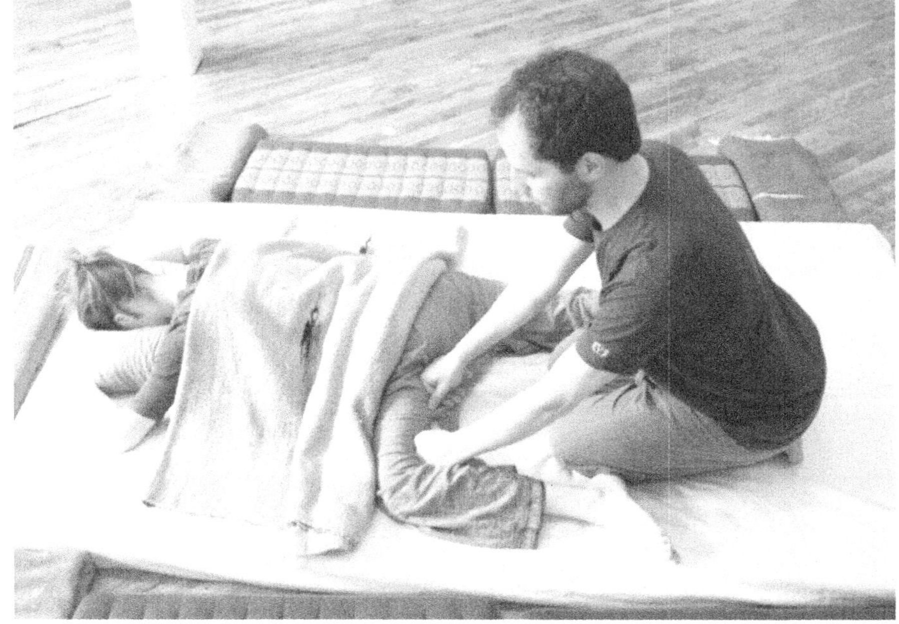

STEP 3: SOFT FIST, ROLLING PIN AND ELBOW MASSAGE

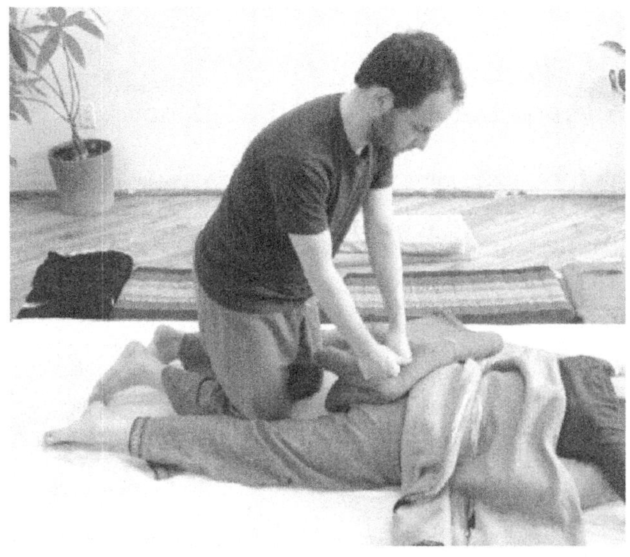

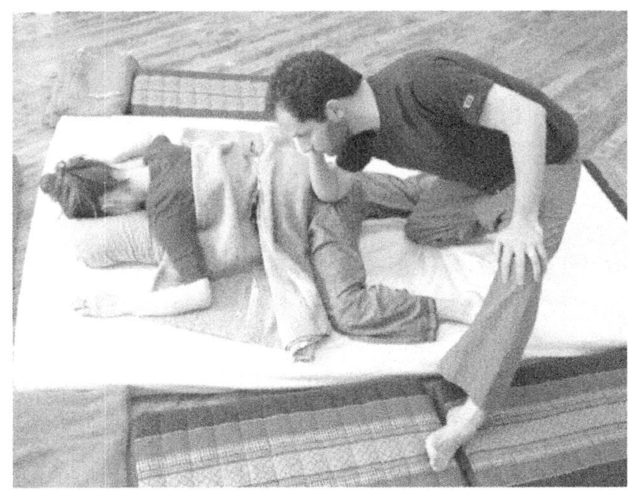

Complete lower body massage using your hands, forearms, and elbows to relax the hip, bum, hamstrings and calves

TRANSITION

- Start in diamond stance behind the left foot
- Raise the foot and come to open warrior
- With 2 hands around the ankle lift the knee, give the leg a shake and put the leg down a couple of inches to the outside
- Turn their foot toward the midline and put your other hand on their knee
- Slide their leg outwards so that it makes a 90° angle

TECHNIQUE

Step 1: Massaging the calf

- 3 options on how to position yourself
    - 1- Diamond facing the calf and if need be put your feet over the straight leg
    - 2- Diamond facing the head
    - 3- Warrior with one knee down on the outside of the straight leg and the foot in between the legs (reserved for when you are taller working on someone much shorter) Use soft fist, palming and thumbing to massage the calf

Complete lower body massage using your hands, forearms, and elbows to relax the hip, bum, hamstrings and calves

TRANSITION

- Start in diamond stance behind the left foot
- Raise the foot and come to open warrior
- With 2 hands around the ankle lift the knee, give the leg a shake and put the leg down a couple of inches to the outside
- Turn their foot toward the midline and put your other hand on their knee
- Slide their leg outwards so that it makes a 90° angle

TECHNIQUE

Step 2: Massaging the hamstrings

- Come to diamond and face the upper leg
- Use soft fist and palming to massage the muscles on the back of the leg taking care to avoid pressing on the bones

Step 2: Use fists and rolling pin to open hip and massage buttocks

- Come up to open warrior
- Use palm over palm to press on the buttocks
- Use rolling pin and elbows to massage the glutes

TRANSITIONING OUT

- Move backwards until you are behind the foot
- Take the ankle and slide their leg until it's straight

BENEFITS

- Massages the calf, hamstrings and back of the leg
- Targets all of the deep muscles of the buttocks
- Hip opener and provides relief to lower back

Tips, Precautions, Making this a Universal Technique

FOR THEIR SAFETY AND COMFORT

With one move you can target the entire lower body in a multitude of ways. There may be some boundary issues working this area of the body, so make choices accordingly. That could include working the calf while your feet are on the other leg as well as the buttocks work. Skip any parts that you think could make your partner uncomfortable. You may want to put a blanket over the buttocks when you massage that area.

For tighter hips you can tuck a rolled up blanket between the mat and their leg to reduce the hip opening effect. You may decide to skip pressing down on the buttocks and simply let gravity do the work for a milder effect. When working on a stiffer person, having the leg in that position for a couple of minutes can already be a very effective hip opener,

These muscles support the back, the upper body and support movements of the legs. As such, by changing the angle, the points of contact and exploring the area inch by inch you will have great results. This is a perfect time to practice awareness and listening to your partner's body, but check in for pressure if you encounter any areas that are particularly tight or tender. For partners with a bad back you may need to skip this technique if it hurts to slide the leg into position.

How slow can you go:

- Start with light pressure
- Slowly sink into deeper muscles and increase the pressure

FOR YOUR SAFETY AND COMFORT

This is a fun technique to give as long as you remember the basics of using your whole body to help. Forward rock is your friend and play with the distance so that you are comfortable especially when rolling and elbowing the buttocks.

ON A BED

- This can be done on a bed or standing next to the bed.

BACK MASSAGE

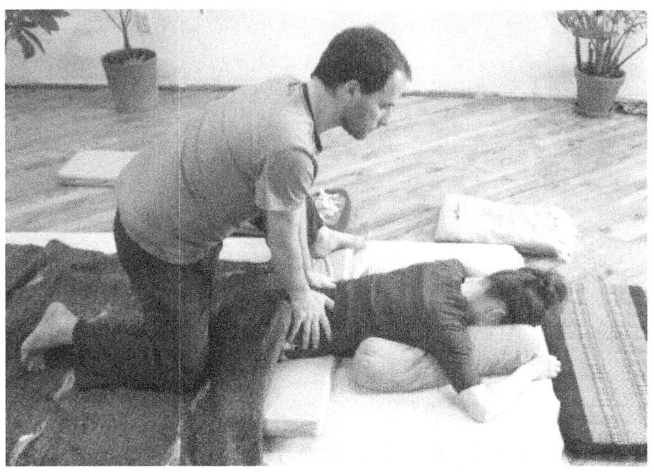

PALMING THE 2 SIDES OF THE BACK

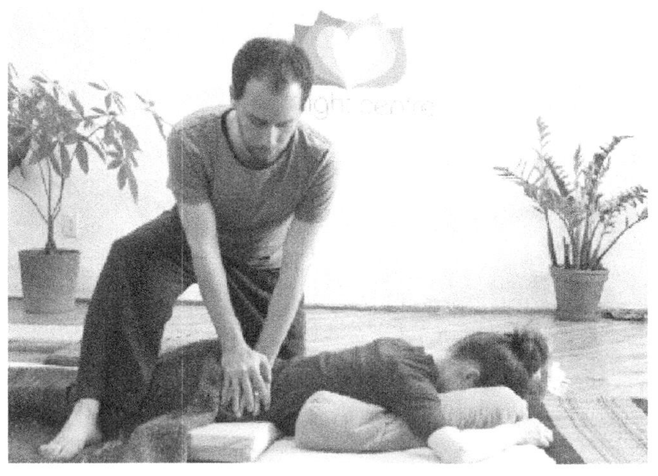

KNEADING THE DOUGH

PALM OVER PALM

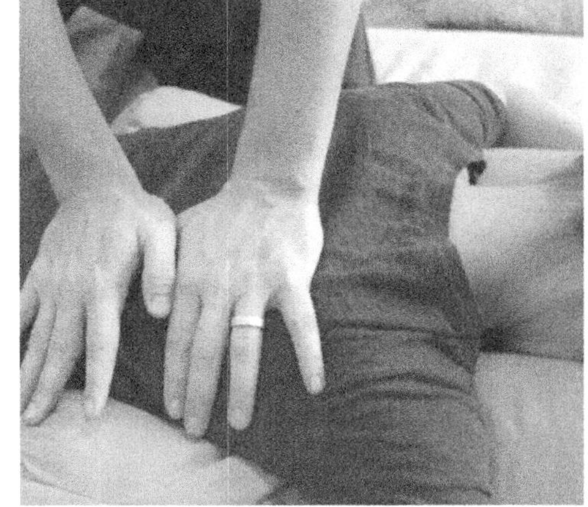

PALM OVER THUMB

TRANSITION

- Position yourself in a warrior stance over the low back facing your partner's head
- You are straddling the back with one knee down on one side and one foot up on the other

TECHNIQUE

Step 1: Massaging both sides of the back at the same time

- Locate the muscles that run parallel to the spine. They run about an inch away from the spine from the lowest part of the back all the way up to the neck
- Place your fists or palms turned out on either side of the spine
- Use side rock to ease into an area

- Repeat with forward rock into the same spot
- Pause, release, repeat moving up and down the back
- You can continue until you are between the shoulder blades

Step 2: Massaging the lower back one side at a time: working the muscles on the far side of the spine

- Position yourself in an elevated open diamond facing the back
- Alternatively you can face the back with a warrior with one foot over the back
- Use forward rock
- Massage the lower back using the kneading dough technique:
    - Place palm over palm
    - Push the muscles away from the spine and use your finger tips to pull the muscles toward the midline.
    - Move from the midline towards the waist and back

Step 3: Massaging one side of the back at a time: working the muscles on the far side of the spine

- Use a combination of palm over palm, soft fists, palm hopping and thumb over thumb to push the muscles away from the spine
- Choose your technique and push the muscles down and away from the spine

TRANSITION

- Spend extra time around the shoulder blades and any other spots of tension making circles and intuitively sinking into areas of greater need
- Draw the arms by their side and massage the shoulders and neck
- Sweep it out

BENEFITS

- Sweet relief for the back and shoulders
- Massages the internal organs
- Expands the breath and ribcage

Tips, Precautions, Making this a Universal Technique

FOR THEIR SAFETY AND COMFORT

How slow can you go:

Giving a great back massage is all about taking your time, listening with full body awareness, communicating and repeat, repeat, repeat. Once you find an area that needs greater attention begin with circles and rocking to ease in the pressure. Increase the pressure ever so slowly, paying attention to their body's signals that they are able to relax while the pressure deepens. If you sense muscles tightening, breath changing, or if you roll off the muscles you will be ready to respond immediately by easing up on the pressure.

If you're unsure of the pressure or what you feel, then be sure to check in with your partner. Ask them where they want the most attention and then also take time to explore the surrounding areas.

If you find an area that needs more attention it is a fine balance between massaging and over massaging. Our recommendation is to work the area for a little while and then move to another part of the back or switch sides and then come back to the area again once or twice more.

One thing to keep in mind is that the greatest results happen when the body is in rest. Our job is to facilitate the body's natural capacity to heal itself. We massage and stretch to bring awareness to a certain area, but it is during rest time that the body renews and repairs itself. As a result, giving tender areas a short break before returning to do a little more work is a great way to go.

When massaging the neck and the tops of the shoulders it's important to bring the arms along the body so those muscles are at rest and sink in slowly with your fingertips and thumbs taking care not to squeeze too tightly on those sensitive muscles.

FOR YOUR SAFETY AND COMFORT

Small adjustments to your stance and alternating between kneeling diamond and warrior are essential so that you are always comfortable and facing your work. It is always worth stopping what you are doing to make these subtle adjustments. When you can massage in greater comfort, then that is exactly what comes through your hands, your body and all your energy.

Massaging with a palm over palm, palm over thumb etc. means that your bottom hand acts as a massage tool feeling the precise spot that needs attention. Once you've found it, keep that hand relaxed. Your top hand acts as the power hand applying pressure. Similarly, it is important to stay elevated with your shoulder over your arms so that your body is there to help out your arms.

ON A BED

- This can be done on a bed either by standing next to the bed or in a comfortable stance such as elevated open diamond or warrior

GETTING READY FOR DOUBLE LEG MASSAGE

- Ask you partner to turn onto their back
- Ask if they would like a pillow under their head
- Have a second pillow nearby which you'll need for "The Sweet Ending"

CHAPTER 7: Double Leg Massage

DOUBLE DUTCH

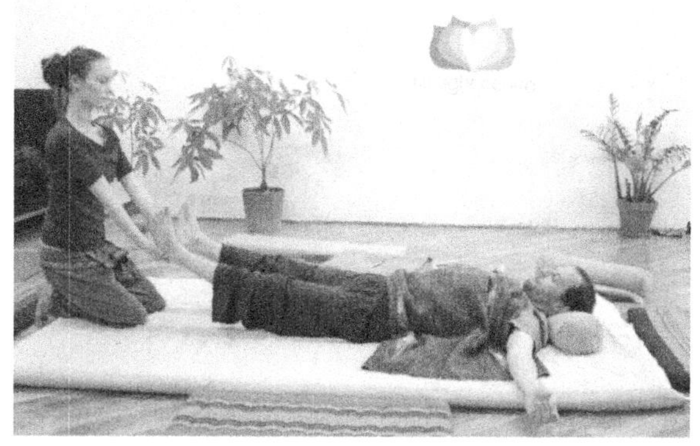

Preparing to raise the legs

Having your arms straight and keeping them straight until standing is the key to lifting heavy legs

Pause and ground at each interval

Playfully shake out the legs and at the same time this is a great way to relax the lower back

TRANSITION

- Sit in a diamond behind the feet of your partner
- Scoop up the heels and place on your lap
- Give the legs a little shake to help relax their back and lower body
- Elevate to kneeling diamond and simultaneously raise the legs up making a circle so that your arms are straight and fingers point up to the ceiling
- Keeping your arms straight and transition to warrior
- Push on their legs and come up to Tai chi stance
- Remain standing and step back so that you are standing comfortably
- Your partner's legs are in your hands by your side
- It can feel as though you are giving yourself a neck, shoulder and arm massage as the weight of their legs provides a lengthening in your body

How slow can you go:

- Simply holding the legs in your hands for a few moments can be very therapeutic and relaxing in cases of very stiff backs.

- Continue slowly and carefully and check in to make sure your partner is comfortable.

In many instances this is a fun and easy way to relax the body

FOR YOUR SAFETY AND COMFORT

Our first task with double leg stretches is to make it as easy as possible to raise and hold legs which are the heaviest part of the body. Good body mechanics are therefore essential to make it easy for you. There is no perfect solution for everyone so it is a good idea to experiment to see what is most comfortable for you. That being said, as a general rule I have found that getting your arms straight and keeping them straight as you cycle through your stances to raise the legs is what works best for most students.

This allows you to rely on technique more than power. Sometimes students will rush through the stances to get from diamond to Tai Chi stance as quickly as they can. This may be a variation for you to try, but I would prefer you take a measured approach where you pause for a moment at each stance to reset and feel grounded.

A very simple alternative to raising the legs would be to stand up and ask your partner to raise their legs and then take them in the palms of your hands.

Once you have the legs raised, think of your body as you shake and make choices that feel like you are giving yourself a massage of the neck and shoulders as you massage your partner.

Some of those choices include:

- Finding the right distance so you are able to stand straight
- Have the feet resting in the palms of your hands
- Only spend as much time in this technique as is comfortable for you.
- It does require some arm strength to do double leg massage, so it may be best to avoid when your partner is bigger than you

ON A BED

- One thing you can do at this point is to pick up the legs so they are slightly off the bed and give them a good shake
- You can stand behind the bed or sit in diamond holding the legs in the palm of your hands for the leg shake
- Generally, it is best to skip the next two double leg stretches (Half Plow and Butterfly) when on a bed and continue with the Hip Swirl

HALF PLOW

First variation: Knees bent targets lower back

2nd variation: Legs straight for hamstrings

Bring the legs up over the body to stretch the legs and back

TRANSITION

- From Double Dutch step back as is necessary so as to rotate your fingers up to the ceiling and push on the heels
- Your arms can be bent as you come closer to their body

TECHNIQUE

There are two ways to do this stretch: With your partner's legs bent will target the lower back and having their legs straight targets the hamstrings.

Variation 1: Legs bent (for lower back)

- Push on their heels so their knees bend
- Forward Rock and push the feet forward
- Release by rocking backwards and repeat

Variation 2: Legs straight (for hamstrings)

- Step back to straighten their legs
- Forward rock, pushing on their heels keeping their legs straight
- Release by rocking backwards and repeat

BENEFITS

- Stretches and lengthens the lower back, sacrum and hips
- Stretches the hamstrings and legs
- Circulates blood to the head

Tips, Precautions, Making this a Universal Technique

FOR THEIR SAFETY AND COMFORT

This technique and all inversions where the legs are elevated is contraindicated for partners with high blood pressure that is not under control, as well as for pregnant women.

The notion that we have legs and a back is a learned human concept, but no one ever told that to our body. In many ways the lower back, hips and upper legs are one unit responsible for many of our daily functions including sitting, walking, climbing and all basic movements. As such when you stretch both legs simultaneously, you are also adding a powerful and therapeutic back massage to the session.

As the practitioner you need to look at the target of each technique in this trifecta of hips, legs and back and modify or choose the variations that customize the technique for your partner. The half plow can therefore be done with legs straight when we want to target the hamstrings and to some degree the large muscles of the lower and mid back. When the legs are bent and the lower back is rounded and rocking you target the lower back, the sacrum and the hips.

How slow can you go:

- Start with the version where they have less issues. If unsure, start with legs bent
- Begin with a small forward rock and shorter pauses
- Increase the stretch as needed and add longer pauses as well
- Continue with the second variation
- If you feel their legs shaking then back up to reduce the stretch

FOR YOUR SAFETY AND COMFORT

The easiest way to hold their legs up is to push on the back of the heels as you transition and as you put your partner in the stretch

ON A BED

- Not advised to do on a bed

BUTTERFLY

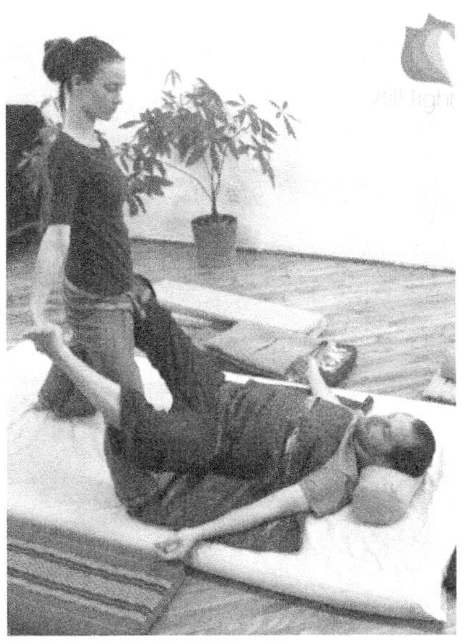

Use Horse Riding stance to bend each leg

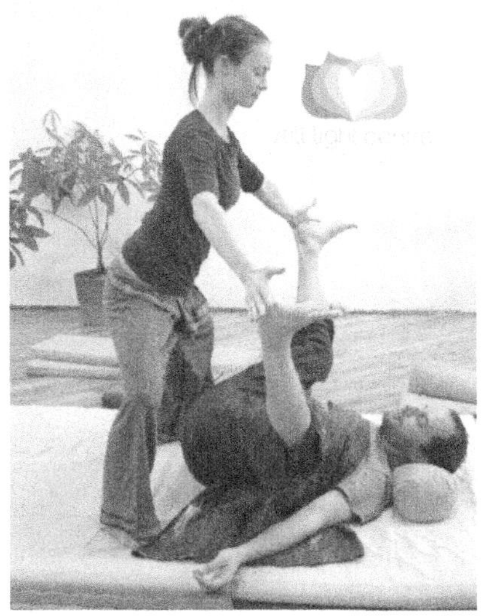

Push the feet forward to round the lower back

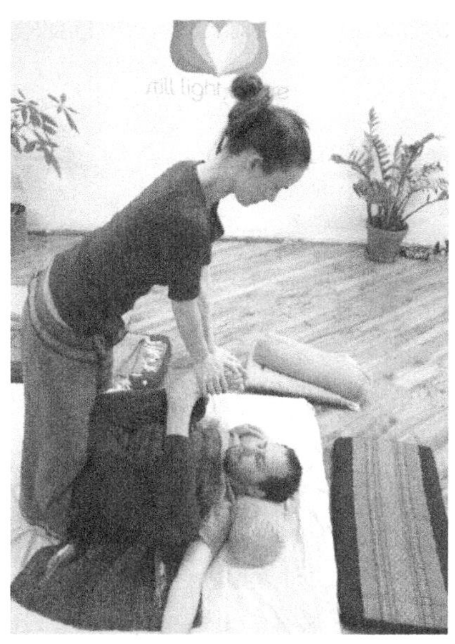

Join the feet together over the center of the body for a hip opener and back stretch

TRANSITION

- Repeat Double Dutch to relax their back
- Holding the back of your partner's heels, open the legs wide
- Use Horse Riding Stance by taking a big step forward with your right leg using it to bend their leg
- Take a big step forward with your left leg using it to bend their other leg

- Push their feet forward so their lower back rounds and comes off the mat

- Circle their legs together in as wide a circle as possible and join their feet together while the knees stay apart

JOIN THE FEET TOGETHER OVER THE BODY AND THE KNEES STAY APART

- At the same time shift your hands from holding the heels to holding the sides of the feet

- Adjust your stance by standing straighter, coming a little closer and hugging their hips with your legs

TECHNIQUE

- Press straight down on the feet so that they come closer to the body

- Use greater repetition and quicker pauses for less flexible partners

- Use longer holds and two or three repetitions for more flexible partners

BENEFITS

- Opens the hips

- Stretches the lower back and sacrum area

- Stretches the legs

Tips, Precautions, Making this a Universal Technique

FOR THEIR SAFETY AND COMFORT

There are 4 options for where their legs will end up once you join the feet together

1) The stiffest partners will not be able to keep their feet together and knees apart. In those cases it is best to go back and use the Half Plow with knees bent. For these people, it will also be received as a hip opener

2) Over the abdomen for partners with very tight hips, legs and back

3) Over the center of the body when there is some tightness in their hips and hamstrings

4) Over the nose for partners with little to no resistance

If you're having difficulty getting their legs into position ask your partner to help you bring their feet together and knees apart and then check in to make sure they are comfortable.

When you are able to hold this stretch for longer periods of time -30-60 seconds- it will target the ligaments of the lower back and is simply a great way to relax the back. However, that would be reserved for your more flexible partners.

How slow can you go:

- Once the feet are in position begin with a small push and short pauses

- Check in for pressure and make any adjustments including giving a deeper stretch and longer pauses of 5 seconds or more- all the way up to 60 seconds for very flexible partners

FOR YOUR SAFETY AND COMFORT

This transition may take some practice in order for it to feel at ease because you are using your legs to help bend their legs. You want to take a big enough step in the horse riding so that your leg presses into their upper leg which will allow their knee to bend. Once you have accomplished that your next task is to get into a comfortable position to support their hips and lower back while you press down on their feet.

Typically, most practitioners will be able to have their arms and back straight as they press down. In some cases your legs will be straight, in others they will be bent slightly, but avoid being in a squat which is just extra work for your back. If you find it difficult to get the legs into position then ask your partner to help you. Describe that you want to bring their feet together, their knees apart and the lower back comes off the ground.

ON A BED

- Not advised to do on a bed

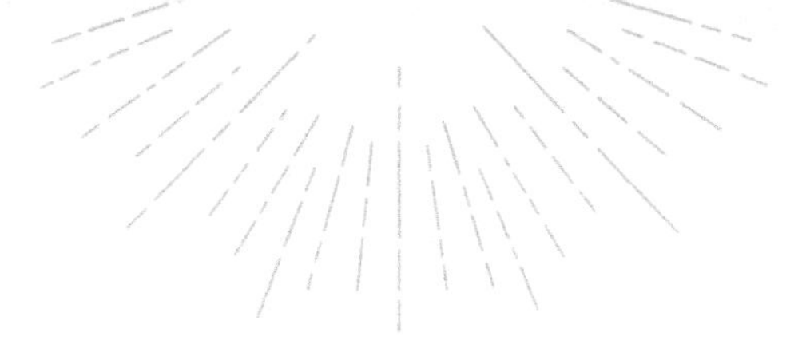

HIP SWIRL

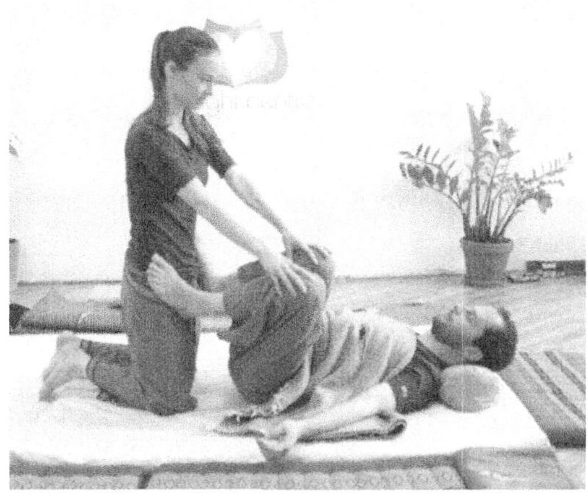

Step 1: Circle Legs on your body

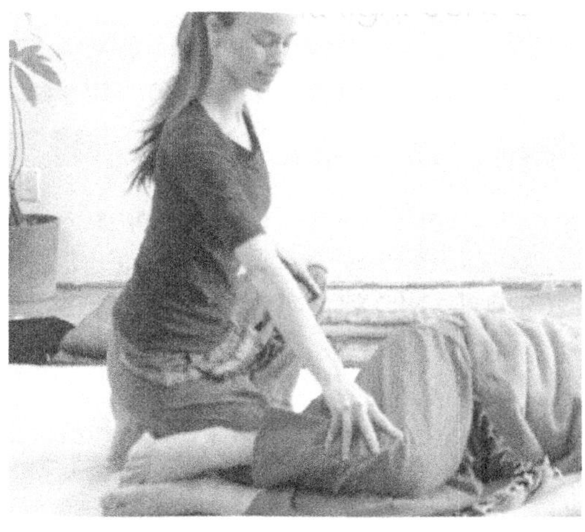

Step 2: Add a gentle twist

Circling the legs to encourage relaxation in the back, hips and legs

TRANSITION

- Hold their feet
- Come to kneeling diamond and bend their knees (or ask them to bend their knees)
- Come close to their body and shift your hands so you hold onto their knees

TECHNIQUE

- Use whirlpool rock to circle the legs
- Pause for a gentle twist with the knees at either side of the body

BENEFITS

- Relaxes the lower back, legs and hips

Tips, Precautions, Making this a Universal Technique

FOR THEIR SAFETY AND COMFORT

Have a pillow or two nearby. As you place them to the side, place a pillow if needed to close any gaps. That could include between their knees, and/or between the ground and their knees.

How slow can you go:

- Start with smaller circles and gradually open up the rotation.
- Pause as you bring the knees side to side
- Palm the legs in the twist for more flexible partners

FOR YOUR SAFETY AND COMFORT

You guide the movement with your hands on their knees and if it feel advantageous you can also place their feet on your front hips. The rest is up to you to decide what feels easiest.

ON A BED

- This is one double leg stretch that you can do on a bed.
- You will need to get on the bed and put yourself in kneeling diamond or if you are standing have your partner slide down to the bottom of the bed so you can reach their knees

TRANSITIONING TO HEAD & NECK MASSAGE- THE SWEET ENDING

- Elevate their knees and lengthen their back by placing a pillow(s) or bolster under their knees
- Place a blanket over their body

CHAPTER 8: Head & Neck Massage - The Sweet Ending

LONG STRETCH

Raise the arms above the head for a nice long stretch

TRANSITION

- Bring their arms up over their head
- Come to kneeling diamond close to the head
- Interlace thumbs in the 'Hey Man' or 'Hey Girl' grip with thumbs interlaced

TECHNIQUE

- Sit in diamond and lean back slightly
- Repeat
- Finish by putting the arms alongside the body

BENEFITS

- Stretches the arms and shoulders
- Relaxes the back

Tips, Precautions, Making this a Universal Technique

FOR THEIR SAFETY AND COMFORT

This technique is contraindicated if your partner cannot raise their arms above their head. You can do this with one arm, if only one arm rises above the head.

Be aware of your grip and make sure not to squeeze too hard as this can be uncomfortable on the thumbs.

HOW SLOW CAN YOU GO

- Begin with 2 or 3 repetitions with short pauses of 1-2 seconds
- Continue with longer pauses of 3-5 seconds

FOR YOUR COMFORT

You are relying on gravity and movement to help with this stretch, as such it should be natural and easy for your body.

You can come into a squat instead of kneeling diamond if you don't have something handy to put under your knees.

ON A BED

- You can do this on a bed as long as there is enough room to put yourself behind their head
- You can also stand behind the bed

SHOULDER WALK

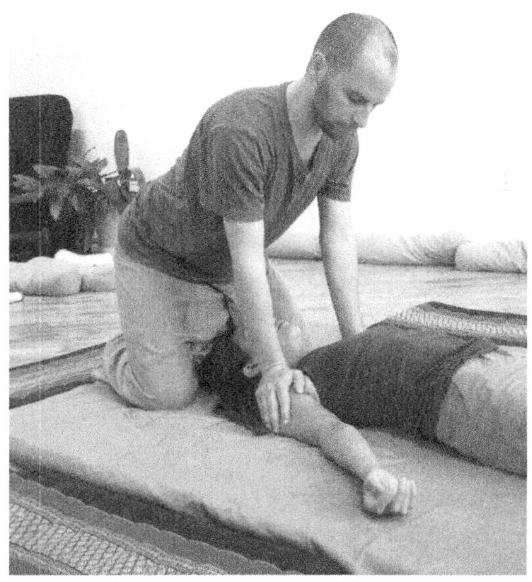

Using your palms to massage the front of the shoulders

TRANSITION

- Make sure their arms are by their side
- Position yourself in elevated kneeling diamond
- Place your palms on the front of either shoulder where they can sink in to soft tissue

TECHNIQUE

- Stretches the arms and shoulders
- Relaxes the back

BENEFITS

- Stretches and relaxes the shoulders and upper chest

Tips, Precautions, Making this a Universal Technique

FOR THEIR SAFETY AND COMFORT

This is a great way to stretch the shoulders and upper chest creating space in tight areas and using minimum effort with your palms. Imagine a band going from one shoulder to the other. We don't want the band to be too pulled too tight. Start by pressing one shoulder at a time. If your partner has very rounded shoulders and lots of pain and tightness in the upper back and neck then press only on one side at a time.

HOW SLOW CAN YOU GO

- Begin with 1 shoulder at a time with short pauses of 1-2 seconds
- Continue with longer pauses of 3-5 seconds
- Press into both shoulders at the same time –only if it is comfortable for your partner

FOR YOUR COMFORT

You are relying on a forward rock to help with this stretch, as such it should be natural and easy for your body. Try to keep your shoulders over your palms- so rock up off of your feet.

ON A BED

- You can do this on a bed as long as there is enough room to put yourself behind their head

- You can also stand behind the bed or sit on a solid chair

HEAD, NECK, SHOULDER AND FACE MASSAGE

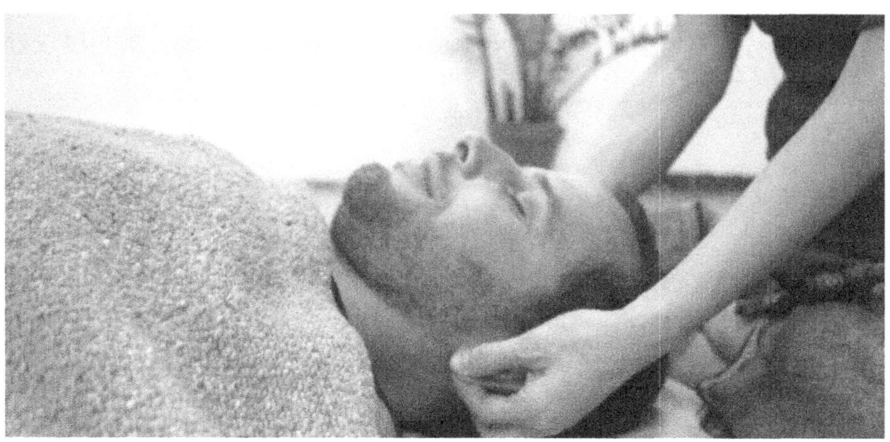

A series of techniques for a blissful head massage to bring your massage to completion

- Sanitize your hands
- Sit comfortably behind their head

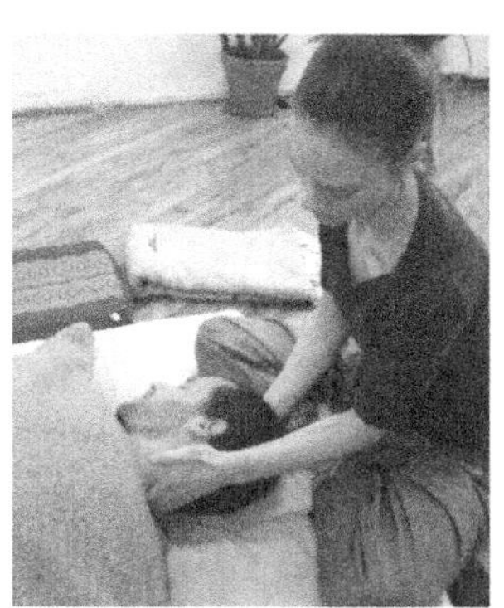

TECHNIQUE
Shoulder & Neck – 1 side

ROCK
Forward

NOTES

- Turn head to 1 side
- Slide 2 fingers onto muscles between scapula and spine
- Make circles on back of shoulder, side of neck up to the ear
- Guide head to the other side & repeat

TECHNIQUE
Shoulder & Neck – 2 sides
ROCK
Forward

NOTES

- Slide both hands as far as possible on back of shoulders
- Push up and repeat
- Circle both sides of neck

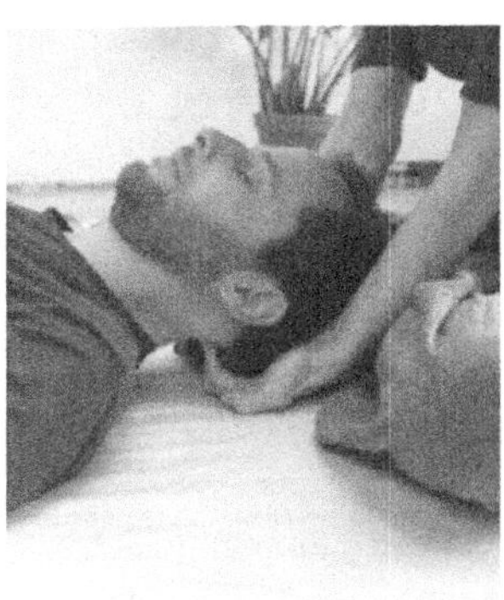

TECHNIQUE
Head in hands
ROCK
Forward
NOTES

- Massage the occipital ridge where the head meets the neck

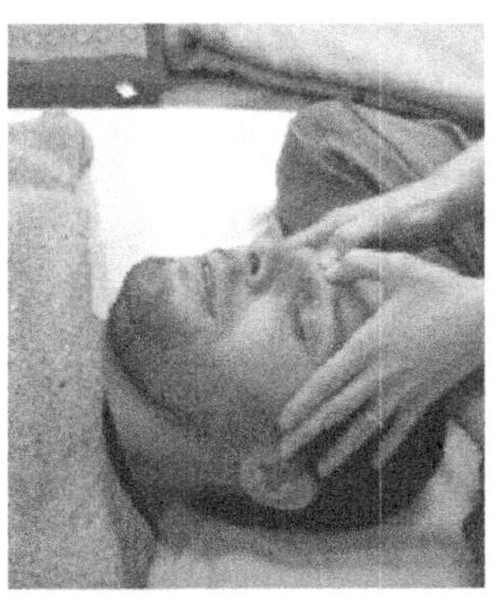

TECHNIQUE
Face Massage
ROCK
Forward
NOTES

- Slide thumbs along the forehead finishing with light circles on temple
- Slide thumbs on cheeks from nose to temples
- Circle the jaws

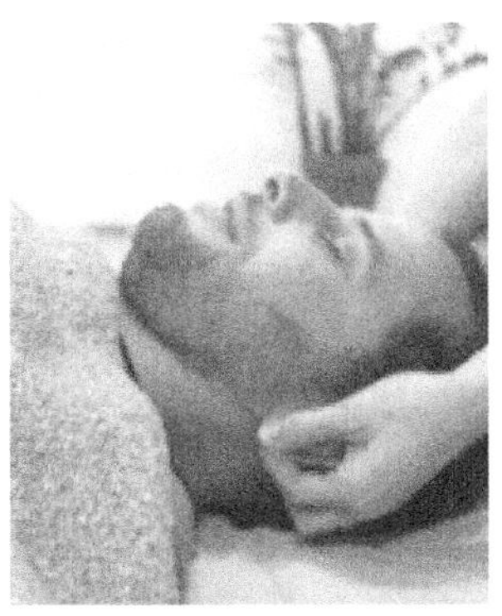

TECHNIQUE
Ear Massage
ROCK
Forward
NOTES

- Circle and squeeze the ridge of ear and lobes
- Circle behind the ears

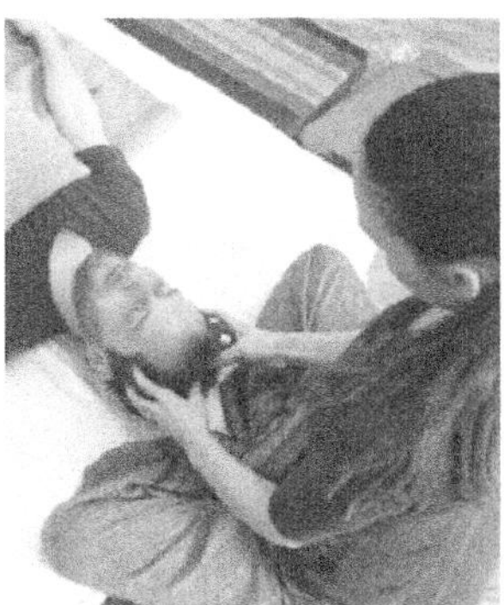

TECHNIQUE
Shampoo
ROCK
Forward
NOTES

- Circle and lightly press points all along the scalp

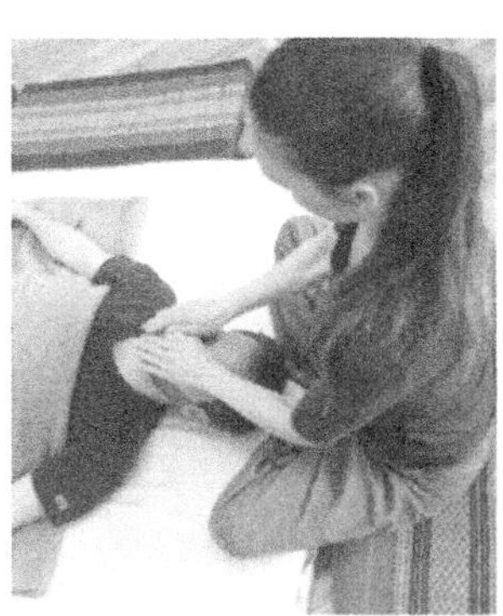

TECHNIQUE
Finishing moves
ROCK
Forward
NOTES

- Rub your hands together and hold over eyes
- Sweep neck and head
- Lean in for a kiss (optional)

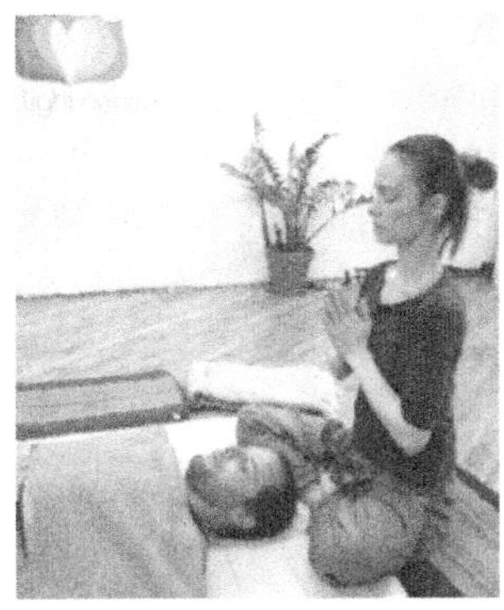

TECHNIQUE
Namaste

BENEFITS

- Deeply relaxing end to your massage

Tips, Precautions, Making this a Universal Technique

FOR THEIR SAFETY AND COMFORT

In this position your head is directly over theirs so be aware of where your breath is going so as not to breathe into their face. The end of the massage can be a very sensitive time as you are both in a place of relaxation and stillness. As such it is important to respect energetic boundaries as well. If you are massaging your partner then it can be a romantic way to end by leaning in for a kiss and giving a hug. When massaging other friends and family, putting your attention on thoughts of gratitude and positivity is a great way to end the session

FOR YOUR COMFORT

This is the time to connect in metta, appreciation, love and joy with your partner and with universal energy. And once your massage is done internally feel the massage being over so you can let go of any stagnant energy or stress that you may have taken on. Release it to the universe and come back into your body. Another way to let go of any unwanted energy is by washing your hands right away and imagine that energy going down the drain.

ON A BED

- You can do this on a bed as long as there is enough room to put yourself behind their head

- You can also stand behind the bed or sit on a solid chair

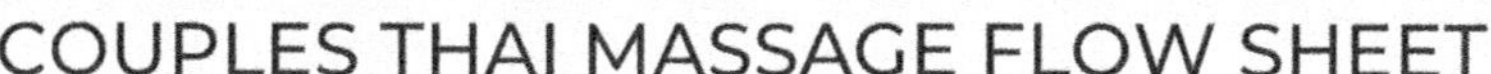

COUPLES THAI MASSAGE FLOW SHEET

SIDE LYING MASSAGE	
1.Palming the Arms	Notes
2.Neck & Shoulder Massage	
3.Back Pedal	

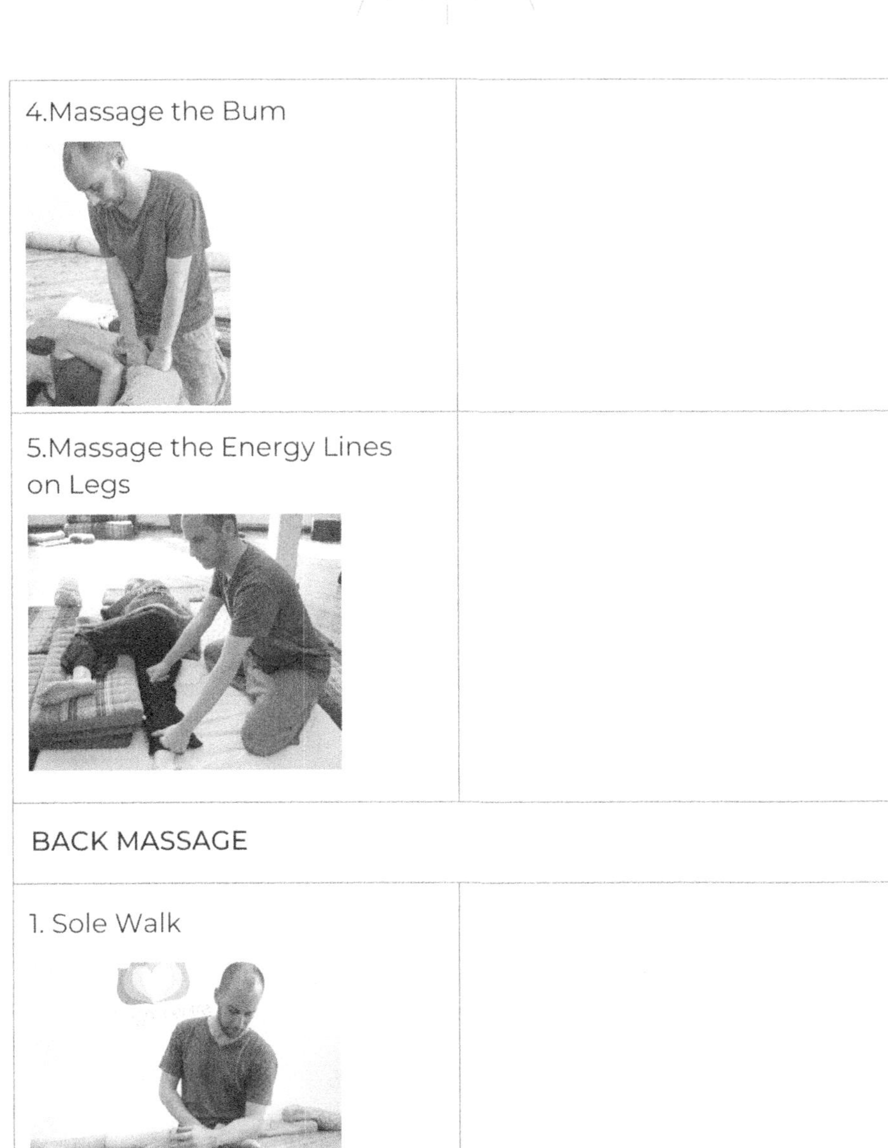

4.Massage the Bum	
5.Massage the Energy Lines on Legs	
BACK MASSAGE	
1. Sole Walk	

2. Calf Roll 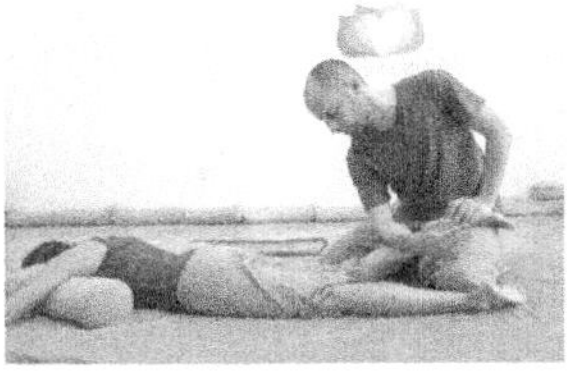	
3. Frog 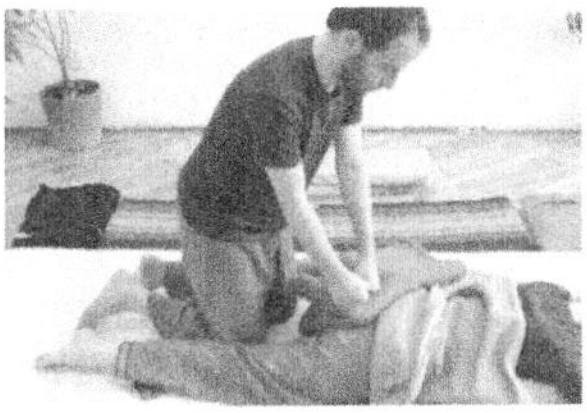	
4. Back Massage 2 sides 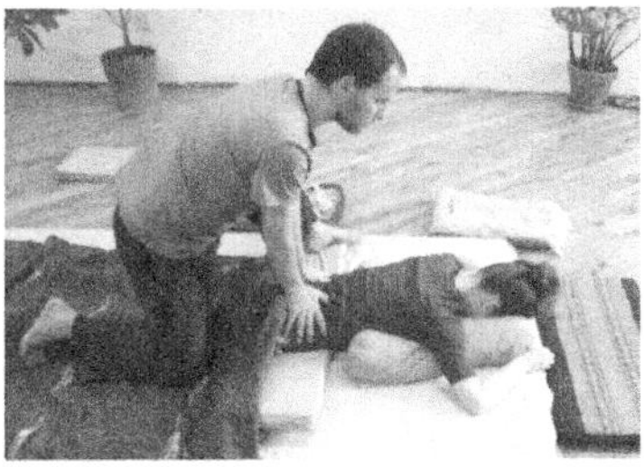	• Palm • Fist

5. Back Massage 1 Side 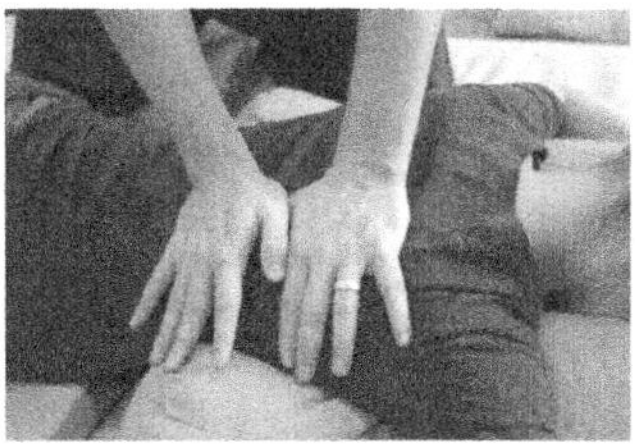	
DOUBLE LEG MASSAGE	
1. Double Dutch 	
2. Half Plough 	

3. Butterfly 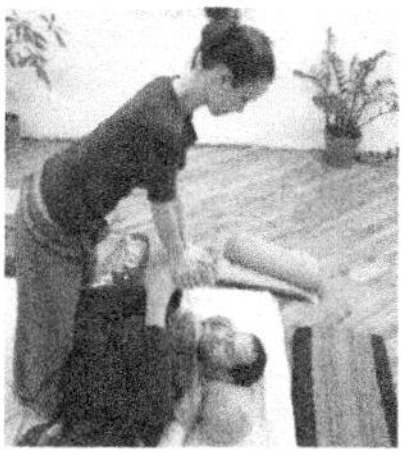	
4. Hip Swirl n' Twist 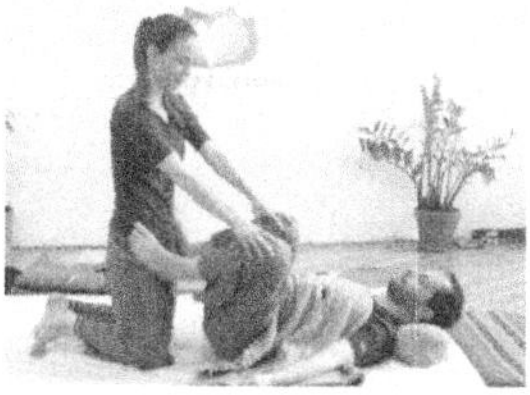	
HEAD & NECK MASSAGE- THE SWEET ENDING	
1. Long Stretch 	

2. Shoulder Walk 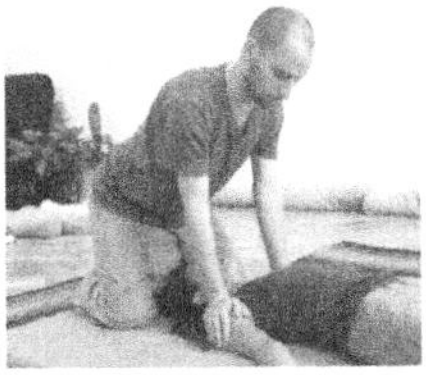	
HEAD MASSAGE:	
1. Shoulder & Neck 1 side 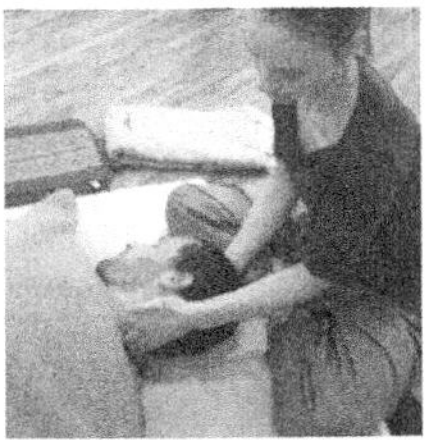	
2 Shoulder & Neck 2 sides 	

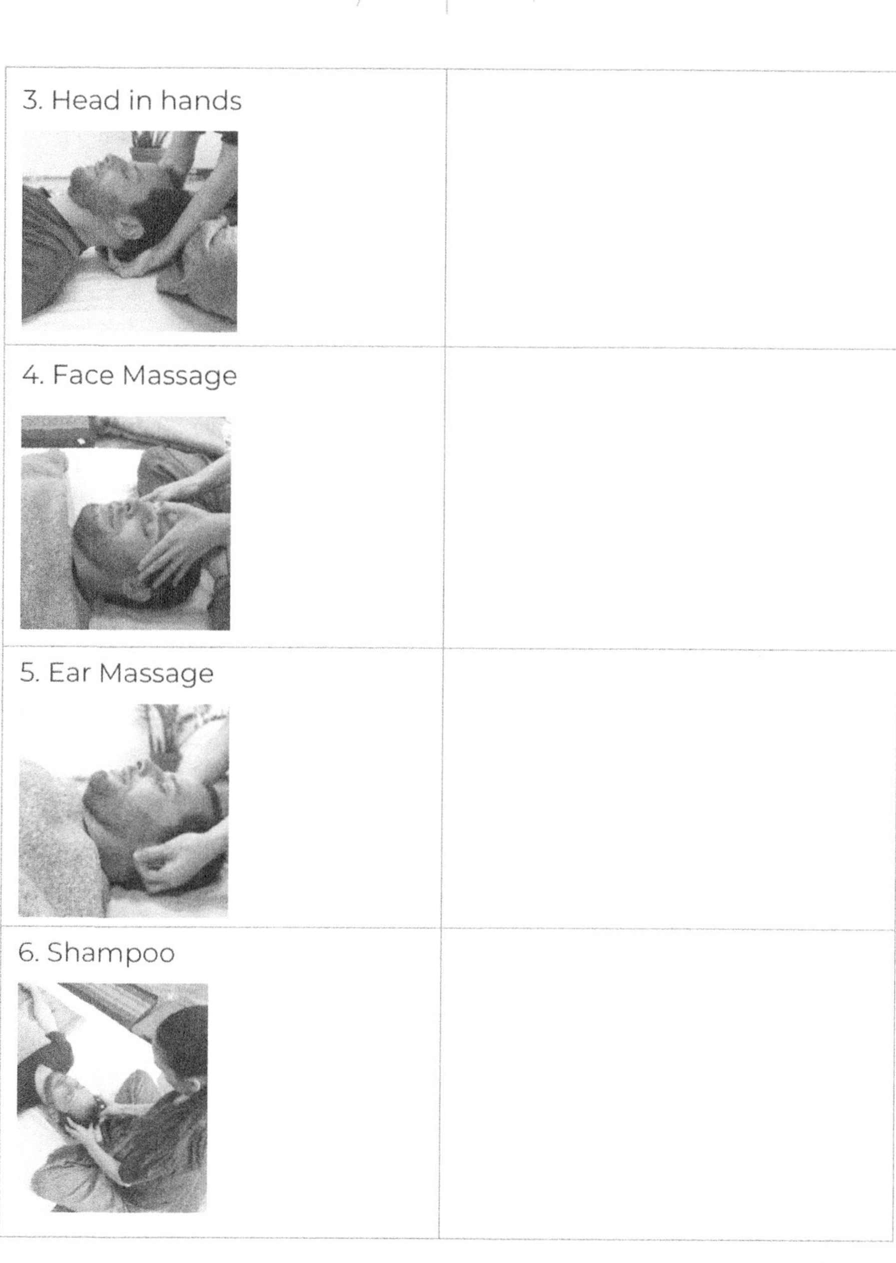

3. Head in hands	
4. Face Massage	
5. Ear Massage	
6. Shampoo	

COUPLES THAI MASSAGE VIRTUAL COURSE

TAKE YOUR MASSAGE TO THE NEXT LEVEL!

Learn Couples Thai Massage and everything in this book with our online course.

- ✓ Step-by-step guidance
- ✓ Done-for-you massages to share from 15 min. up to 1 hour
- ✓ Incredible support
- ✓ Visit https://www.stilllightcenter.com/online-massage-courses or email info@stilllightcenter.com to get started

ABOUT THE AUTHOR

Shai Plonski has taught Thai Massage to more than 11,000 people on three continents for the past 20 years. He has written or co-written 17 books and manuals on the art of this practice. Shai loves educating other people on how giving massage is a life-changing choice and sharing how simple and easy it is to do.

Shai is the founder of the Still Light Center School of Thai Massage. Our school is for people looking to massage professionally or with loved ones and family members. Our system is designed to teach you a quality massage in the quickest time possible and then further support your deeper immersion.

We make our own best-selling Thai Massage mat, have written three best-selling books along with a suite of manuals designed to take you by the hand and guide you through every step of becoming an outstanding practitioner.

You have the choice to learn Thai Yoga Massage online or in person Shai's home base is in Berkeley and San Francisco.

We also teach certification courses on retreat (including the Kripalu Center) and yoga studios across North America and around the world.

Still Light Center courses are accredited with NCBTMB, CMTO, Yoga Alliance, NHPCanada & CMTNB for continuing education. We are an accredited vocational school with the province of Ontario.

To learn more visit: https://www.stillightcenter.com

CONNECT WITH SHAI

Thank you so much for making the time to read this book and bringing Compassionate Couples Thai Massage into your life and those you care for. I'm excited for you to start your path of giving massage and how it will help to improve your health and your sessions.

If you have any questions, feel free to contact me at https://www.stilllightcenter.com

Connect with me on Facebook: https://www.facebook.com/shaiplonski/

Check out my massage blog and the latest updates by visiting: http://www.stilllightcenter.com

I publish new videos on YouTube every week: https://www.youtube.com/shaiplonski

You can also check me out on Instagram: https://www.instagram.com/shaiplonski/?hl=en

Wishing you incredible massages, health and happiness- now and everyday

Much love,
Shai

OTHER BOOKS BY SHAI PLONSKI

- ✓ Thai Massage: Unlocking the Secrets to Universal Touch
- ✓ The Joy of Giving Massage: How to Give a Massage so Good You'll Want to do it All the Time
- ✓ Table Thai Massage: 3 Hours of Techniques to Radically Transform Your Massage
- ✓ Thai Massage for Pregnancy and the Elderly: The Soft Approach
- ✓ Thai Massage for Restorative Yoga Teachers

These books and more Thai Massage manuals are available by visiting https://www.stilllightcenter.com

ONE LAST THING...

Thank you for reading! If you enjoyed this book or found it useful, I'd be very grateful if you'd post a short review on Amazon. I read every comment personally and am always learning how to make this book even better. Your support really does make a difference.

Search for Couples Thai Massage by Shai Plonski to leave your review.

Thanks again for your support!

Made in the USA
Middletown, DE
27 July 2023